Praise f
Hope, Not

T0279125

"Really enjoyed it; beautifully written and quite fascinating."
—Jonathan Kellerman, bestselling author

"Perhaps it seems incongruous to speak of 'enjoying' a book on such a serious topic, but I must say that I have found these words profound, inspiring, and very real. Rabbi Blech has tapped into a vein of reflection that our culture shies away from, and has addressed the reality of death with gentleness, wisdom, and an evident faith. The author has a gift for blending ancient insights with a deep sensitivity to our modern culture, his own personal situation, and a great deal of gentle humor."
—Murray Watson, vice-rector, St. Peter's Seminary

"I read *Hope, Not Fear* and learned quite a bit. I was struck by the similarities between Judaism and Islamic traditions. Rabbi Blech's personal anecdotes from his long and illustrious career are enlightening and informative. The extensive discussion regarding near death experience is very edifying."
—Faroque Ahmad Khan, chair, board of trustees, Islamic Center of Long Island

"This is an intelligent and soulful exploration of the unknowable. Rabbi Blech doesn't try to conquer death or 'spin' it or sugarcoat it. He's amazed by death, but not fazed by it. He looks it squarely in the eye, turns it around, peels back the layers, and, ultimately, infuses it with meaning. Blech finds meaning in death by discerning divine meaning in life. If God is eternal, and we are created in God's image, then we share in that eternity. Our physical bodies might die, but our little piece of God—our individual souls—never dies. Our souls live on in everything we have done in this life, in every person we have touched, every word we have shared, every song we have sung. Living with that awareness helps us fulfill our purpose in life."
—David Suissa, publisher and editor-in-chief, *Jewish Journal*

HOPE, NOT FEAR

A Guide to Changing the Way We View Death

Rabbi Benjamin Blech

ROWMAN & LITTLEFIELD
Lanham • Boulder • New York • London

Published by Rowman & Littlefield
An imprint of The Rowman & Littlefield Publishing Group, Inc.
4501 Forbes Boulevard, Suite 200, Lanham, Maryland 20706
www.rowman.com

86-90 Paul Street, London EC2A 4NE

British Library Cataloguing in Publication Information Available

Library of Congress Cataloging-in-Publication Data

Names: Blech, Benjamin, author.
Title: Hope, not fear : A Guide to Changing the Way We View Death /
    Rabbi Benjamin Blech.
Description: Lanham : Rowman & Littlefield, [2018] | Includes
    bibliographical references and index.
Identifiers: LCCN 2018012698 (print) | LCCN 2018020651 (ebook) |
    ISBN 9781538116654 (electronic) | ISBN 9781538116647 (cloth :
    alk. paper) | ISBN 9798881805586 (pbk : alk. paper)
Subjects: LCSH: Death—Religious aspects.
Classification: LCC BL504 (ebook) | LCC BL504 .B54 2018 (print) |
    DDC 202/.3—dc23
LC record available at https://lccn.loc.gov/2018012698

♾™ The paper used in this publication meets the minimum
requirements of American National Standard for Information
Sciences—Permanence of Paper for Printed Library Materials, ANSI/
NISO Z39.48-1992.

To my loving family and friends, who grant me a vision of heaven while I'm still here on earth

CONTENTS

INTRODUCTION

What do you do when you're told you're going to die?

After the initial shock of receiving a death sentence from my doctor, I had to face the reality that we all seek to avoid in spite of its universal inevitability.

None of us wants to believe we are mortal. We live our lives as if we will be around forever.

We can't imagine our nonexistence and so we deny the possibility of our disappearance.

Like Woody Allen, we claim we're not afraid of death, but we "just don't want to be there when it happens"—and we stubbornly persist in believing that we will somehow be the exception to the fate of all humankind.

But life has a way of forcing us to confront bitter truth.

There are many ways in which we can be jolted into recognizing that our days are indeed numbered. It need not be a judicial verdict of execution that ensures life will be cut short. Sickness, infirmities, old age—all equally come as powerful reminders of our transient residence on earth.

My wake-up call came with the medical diagnosis that I have a fatal disease for which at present there is no cure. Like everyone else, I'm going to die—but for me it will probably be sooner rather than later.

And what I discovered in the aftermath of that frightening news is that life takes on a totally different meaning when the idea of death becomes truly relevant and personal.

In some ways, acknowledging mortality is liberating. Mahatma Gandhi famously advised us to "live as if you were to die tomorrow; learn as if you were to live forever." Every moment is more precious when you know it could be your last; every experience is more intense when you're aware that it might never be repeated.

But the flip side all too often is that fear of the unknown is debilitating and depressing. We have no idea what awaits us, and there is still so much here we have left undone. Will we never know what happens to our loved ones; will we never again see our mates or our children?

We wish we knew more about death. And the closer we get to that meeting with the universal mystery, the more urgent our need to define it.

Is death the end or a new beginning? With all of its discoveries, science still hasn't given us the answer. So we are left to wonder and to wait.

My personal confrontation with a fatal diagnosis inspired me to search for meaningful answers. What other avenues to truth are there when scientific criteria based on observation are unavailable? What legitimacy can we assign to the responses of faith as well as to mystical teachings such as those transmitted over thousands of years by Jewish spiritual masters of Kabbalah? What are we to make of recent anecdotal evidence offered by people with near-death experiences who were brought back to life after the cessation of brain activity and heartbeat? Are we any closer to solving the mystery of our mortality and to comprehending our final journey? And most important of all—how can our fears be replaced by a measure of hope and of trust that will allow us to live out the remainder of our days without despair or depression?

No, I haven't found all the answers. But what I did discover has given me a great gift that I want to share with others. I no longer fear death. Even as I treasure every moment of life more than before, I await my end with the certainty beautifully captured by the Roman philosopher Seneca: "The day which we fear as our last is but the birthday of eternity."

What led me to this conclusion is the theme of this book.

I bring to it the special blessings of my career and my life experiences.

Professionally, I have been a rabbi for more than half a century. But let me stress at the outset that this is not a rabbinic book or even a specifically Jewish one, but rather the reflections of a spiritual leader forced to confront personally a universal fear. I've had the opportunity to discuss the insights of the pages that follow with prominent theologians of other faiths—Catholics, Protestants, and Muslims—and been delighted, and in some cases even astounded, by how much fundamental agreement there is among us.

I have counseled hundreds of people in times of despair and loss, and learned much from them as well. Congregants shared with me stories about death and dying, as well as mystical experiences they were too embarrassed to reveal even to close family members for fear of being labeled emotionally unstable. I was often present when people died and can personally verify many of the remarkable claims made by Elisabeth Kübler-Ross, Raymond Moody, and others who have specialized in the study of death and dying.

As a university professor, at first solely attracted to the scholarly writings of purely rational philosophers, I slowly and almost grudgingly developed a fascination for the mystical insights of Kabbalah. From this discipline, far removed from the simplistic

Hollywood version preached by Madonna and other contemporary cultural icons, I discovered some of the most profound truths
about the human condition and why belief in the continued existence of the soul after death is not only reasonable, but highly
probable.

From my faith, rooted in the Bible and its oral traditions that
have accompanied it for millennia, I found the certainty to affirm
that death is but moving from one room to another, from a material existence to a more spiritual reality.

Certain events in my life also played an important part in bringing me to my present understanding of life and death. In the book,
I share with readers moments such as my unexpected meeting as a
young man with Ernest Hemingway in his home in Cuba and the
discussion we had about why heaven and hell aren't explicitly
mentioned in the Bible; my powerfully moving encounter with
Pope John Paul II, which fortified my belief in a heaven open to
the righteous people of all faiths; my discussion with a student in
my Hebrew high school class whose questions almost prophetical-
ly preceded her death by a day; and my fortuitous meeting with a
priest at the airport in Dallas that taught me the importance of the
Jewish mission, in the words of Isaiah, to be "a light unto the
nations."

All of these moments, in concert, confirmed my belief that God
in His infinite goodness wanted to prepare me for my final passage
by affording me a somewhat prophetic glimpse into the mystery of
what awaits us.

This book is reminiscent of another rabbi who some years ago
was moved by personal tragedy to write about another universal
theme that has long troubled most of mankind. Theodicy, why bad
things happen to good people, is one of the two greatest mysteries
of life. No wonder that Harold Kushner's *When Bad Things Happen to Good People*, which describes his efforts to cope with his

son's fatal illness, deservedly became an international bestseller, reaching more than nine million readers.

The only other great mystery that compares in magnitude to the apparent unfairness of life is the enigma of death. We are all going on the journey of our lives without a clear map or a known destination. We all desperately want as much information as possible.

My tragedy is that I've been told I'll be taking the final leg of that trip in the not-too-distant future. My comfort is the knowledge I've sought out and reflected upon in the pages that follow. My prayer is that this book will help others as much as my search for the answers has helped me. And my hope is that I will live long enough to be witness to its positive impact.

I

FACING THE INEVITABLE

For dust thou art, and unto dust shalt thou return.

—Genesis 3:19

I had no warning.

It was just meant to be my annual physical exam. No health problems. No complaints. Both my mother and father lived into healthy old age. I was confident it would be like all the other times. I would receive the usual reassuring words that all was well, coupled with the suggestion that I return in six months to a year.

It seemed strange that when the doctor called me to sit down in his office to provide me with the results of his examinations, he wasn't smiling.

It was then I began to suspect something might be wrong.

"It is hard for me to have to tell you this," he began. "There is no way I can sugarcoat it. You are a rabbi, a man of faith, and I know you will find a way to cope with the dreadful news I must share with you. You have a fatal disease that is extremely rare, and there is no known cure."

I hardly heard the rest of what he was saying.

My head began to spin. I had been the rabbi of a congregation for almost four decades. In my pastoral duties, I counseled the sick and I gave strength to the dying. Most often, I seemed to know what to say to those confronted by the gravest challenges. I helped people face death.

Yet this time it was so totally different.

This wasn't happening to someone else. This was *me*!

And for the first time in my life, even though I was in my late seventies, I realized that I was actually going to die.

How do we forget that truth about our existence? Death is the universal reality of life—yet a fact all of us choose to ignore. We assume we will live forever even though no one has ever accomplished that feat. We expunge the possibility from our minds—as if by denying its inevitability, we can prevent the certainty of its arrival.

We begin our journey to death from the day we are born. But when we are reminded of our final destination, we react with the same kind of shock I expressed in the doctor's office.

The name of my disease is cardiac amyloidosis. Amyloids are proteins that can attack different parts of the body. If they invade the brain, the result is Alzheimer's. When they affect other areas, such as the kidneys or liver, those organs lose their ability to perform their specific functions. My problem is in the heart. The amyloids that shouldn't be there are hardening the muscle, making it more difficult to pump the blood needed for life.

The doctor tried to be reassuring. I tuned him out. I didn't fully listen to the rest of what he told me. I rushed home to Google what the Internet had to teach me about my illness.

That was a big mistake.

After the diagnosis, the first site I came up with declared, with a note of certainty, that a patient usually has six months to live. I soon learned that this information was outdated. There were projections that spoke of the potential of years, not months. And then there was news of stem-cell research and other possible therapies being worked on in laboratories around the world that offered long-range hope.

I came to realize that my diagnosis was not the same as an imminent death certificate. No one could really say with assurance how much longer I had to live.

And then the thought hit me. If my disease didn't carry an expiration date, I wasn't much different from anyone else on earth. Life itself is a fatal disease for which there is no known cure.

Yes, I'm going to die. So is everyone. Will I go sooner rather than later? Perhaps. But who knows?

What the doctor had really confirmed for me with his dire news was simply that I am mortal. And that is something I surely already knew. It is no less than the biblical truth that we come from the dust of the earth and to the dust of the earth we shall return.

Yet receiving a death sentence totally altered my perspective. Death moved from the back of my mind to the forefront of my consciousness. It was no longer some half-acknowledged fear. The thought of death became my daily companion.

And now, ever since the initial diagnosis, I've made an amazing discovery. My companion became my friend. My recognition of mortality has added incredibly positive dimensions to my existence. In many ways, this has been the most fulfilling, most contented, and happiest time of my life.

Realizing as I never did before that the days I have left on earth are limited in number makes me treasure every one of them far more than I ever thought possible. Drawing on the insights I have gained from my studies and from my faith, I do not fear death as the great unknown. I view it, as the Indian philosopher Rabindranath Tagore so beautifully put it, as "putting out the lamp because the dawn has come."

What I have found to my great surprise is that living life with a real awareness of its eventual end can actually be a source of great blessing.

And what I want to do in these pages is to share that blessing with you—to give you the strength to accept your finite existence here on earth and to give you the confidence to await something far more beautiful for eternity.

2

THE COFFIN IN THE SYNAGOGUE

Man is likened to a breath; his days are as a shadow that passeth away.

—Psalms 144:4

On a sunny Friday afternoon some years back, I took a fascinating tour of synagogues in Jerusalem, the holiest city in the world.

Almost all of these houses of worship were very interesting. But one was fascinating in a way that marked it as totally different from all the others.

It was built by Jews who emigrated from somewhere in deepest Africa. They brought with them a fascinating custom that they explained was part of their tradition for almost two thousand years, from the time Jews first conceived of building houses of worship after the destruction of the Temple.

The front wall featured the expected. Like every other congregation, there was an ark behind a beautifully decorated curtain, containing a number of Torah scrolls.

But on the adjacent wall, highlighted by special lighting and built into its surface, was clearly a coffin. Not a make-believe replica, but a real coffin about the size of an average human being.

I knew there could not possibly be a body inside. Jewish law forbids *Kohanim*, descendants of Aaron, brother of Moses—the priestly tribe who to this day still make up a significant number of Jewry—from coming in contact with the dead or even being in the same room with them. It was inconceivable that this was a Jewish version of Westminster Abbey, serving as the final resting place for some prominent ancestor. That would preclude some Jews from entering.

So I asked, what in the world was a coffin doing so prominently displayed in a synagogue?

The elder of the congregation explained it to me.

"We are surprised," he confided, "that your synagogues see no need for something as important as this reminder. You surely know the instruction of the Talmud in the portion of *The Ethics of the Fathers* that we are to constantly consider three things in order to avoid falling into sin. 'Know from where you come, to where you are finally going, and before whom you are destined to give a final accounting. You come from a drop of semen; you are going to the grave; and you will have to justify all the deeds of your life before the Creator.' Awareness of our mortality is the most important truth we must impress upon ourselves every moment in order to live our lives to the fullest."

Gazing at the coffin every day as they occupied themselves with their prayers to God was as much of a wake-up call to them as my medical diagnosis had been for me.

With the wisdom of their ancestors, they had created a visual symbol not of the affirmation of death but of the way in which its recognition could transform life.

To the outsider, it might appear morbid. To those who understood its message, it was a profound statement with a demand for introspection by its viewers.

Knowing that death awaits us helps us to evaluate everything we do in a different way.

By now the oft-quoted line may be a cliché, but it is true. "No one ever said on his deathbed, 'I wish I had spent more time at the office.'"

What is it that people do when they know their days are numbered?

They look back with regret at time foolishly wasted.

They wonder why they didn't spend more time with family and friends.

They question why they expended so much of their efforts acquiring things they now realize they can't take with them and that have no long-lasting value.

They can't understand why they allowed pettiness to undo friendships and why they permitted minor slights to stand in the way of meaningful relationships.

If only they could have stared at a coffin whenever they forgot those things that truly matter. Every day they would have been able to remember the warning of Benjamin Disraeli that life is too short to be little.

We moderns try to deny death as much as possible. We hesitate to even call it by its name. We use euphemisms to suggest that people pass on, pretending they have simply moved away. We say they depart, they leave us, they rest in peace. As if verbal camouflage could undo reality.

If we only had the courage on an ongoing basis to face up to what ultimately awaits us, we might find the same wisdom that those who are critically ill are very often endowed with.

It is not morbid to tell yourself, "I am going to die." It is liberating. It frees you from being enslaved to what in your heart you know doesn't really matter. It permits you to tell yourself that this is not what you would do or how you would act if you had but one day to live. It allows you to break the chains of habit that shackle you merely because you rationalize that they are only temporary. It prevents you from wasting your life while you spend your days preparing to live.

Not such a bad idea, after all, to be forced to face a coffin. And if we have not adopted that custom in our own synagogues, Jews have other moments when tradition commands a comparable ritual.

A *kittel* is the name of the white linen shroud in which, according to Jewish law, we bury the dead. Yet, there are times when a *kittel* is also used by the living.

On the high holy days of Rosh Hashanah and Yom Kippur, the *kittel* is worn by leaders of the congregation as they offer prayers for forgiveness. Jews believe that these days are set aside as days of judgment, when the heavenly court reviews our deeds and decides our fate for the year to come. The *kittel* is a powerful reminder to all to appreciate the seriousness of the moment. As we stand before God during this annual time for divine verdict, we remind ourselves, by way of "the garment of the dead," that the day will come when we will leave this earth, and our entire lives will be evaluated from a heavenly perspective.

The Talmud records the advice of Rabbi Eliezer: "Repent one day before your death." When his disciples asked him the obvious question, "But how will we know which day that is?" he responded, "Exactly. For that reason we must live every day as though it were our last."

We need to live our lives with the constant awareness of our mortality. On the holiest days of the year we find a way to symbolically stress this truth via the very garment reserved for our burial.

A powerful illustration of the message of the *kittel* occurred a few years ago in Jerusalem when Edward Reichmann died after a long illness at the age of eighty. He was a world-renowned Jewish real estate tycoon who passed away after having amassed a vast fortune worth billions of dollars. He left two wills, directing that one be opened immediately and the other thirty days later. Among the instructions left in his first will was the request that he be buried with a certain pair of socks he owned.

The Reichmann children immediately brought the socks to the Chevra Kadisha, the religious functionaries in Jewish communities empowered to make all the necessary funeral arrangements in accordance with Jewish law, requesting that their father be buried in them. The Chevra Kadisha refused, reminding the family that it would be a violation of Halacha, the law that mandates the *kittel* as the sole garment in which the deceased is to be dressed on going to meet his Creator. The children pleaded to be allowed to fulfill their father's wishes, explaining that as a very pious and learned man, he obviously had a very good reason to make this request. The Chevra Kadisha remained firm in their refusal.

The family frantically summoned the Chevra Kadisha to a judicial proceeding before the most respected and learned rabbi in the city. Remarkably, the rabbi affirmed the decision of the burial society. He explained to the children that although their father left that request when he was in this world, now that he was in the world of truth, he surely understood that it was in his best interests to be buried without the socks, in strict accordance with the law.

Mr. Reichmann was buried without his socks. Thirty days later, the second will was opened, and it read: "My dear children, by now you must have buried me without my socks. I wanted you to truly understand that a man can have billions of dollars, but in the end, he can't even take along one pair of socks—only what God decrees is what we may bring with us to the other world. This is what you must always remember after I am certain you have buried me in my *kittel*, the shroud I wore every year on the high holy days in anticipation of my demise."

To live all of our days with the knowledge of the transitory nature of our existence and the folly of devoting our lives merely to the accumulation of more and more possessions is perhaps the most meaningful message to serve as a guide for lives of purpose and fulfillment.

And there is still one more moment aside from the high holy days that Jewish tradition deems appropriate for wearing the *kittel*. It is for an event that, hopefully, happens only once in a lifetime. It seems almost bizarre, and for those who do not understand its purpose, it has been the subject of much misguided merriment. Please don't smirk when I tell you that the *kittel* is the prescribed item of clothing for the groom on his wedding day as he stands under the canopy, the *chuppah*, to sanctify his marriage. More times than I want to remember I've heard the jokes that suggest it's the Jewish way of commemorating the death of a bachelor's freedom. It may be a humorous suggestion, but it is way off the mark in terms of its real religious meaning.

The *kittel* serves a powerful purpose whose message can spell the difference between a marriage destined for success or doomed to failure.

Choosing the identity of our life's partner is probably the most important decision we will ever make. The love that brings two partners together ideally ought to last a lifetime. Whether the words are actually said or not (they're not part of the Jewish religious ritual), the implication of "I do" is "till death do us part." And so a *kittel* affirms that this union is meant to last forever, until the final curtain. It is a symbolic declaration that the newlyweds will fulfill their purpose on earth together and leave a legacy created by a lifetime of love that marks their lives as meaningful.

It is yet another version of the coffin in the synagogue. Even in the happiest of moments, we let a reminder of our mortality sneak in to express our awareness of life's seriousness. We won't take any day for granted; we won't fail to take advantage of any opportunity we have to share and to show our love for each other—because life is too brief to be wasted.

I won't ever forget the terrible price a woman in my congregation continues to pay because, in a moment of anger, she ignored the truth taught by the *kittel*. Before her husband left for work one day, they had a bitter argument. Even those deeply in love can on occasion have strong disagreements. But this time, the fight escalated beyond reason. In a rage, as her husband stood by the door, she yelled out, "I hope you drop dead and never come back."

And that is exactly what he did.

He made it as far as the Long Island Railroad station and then dropped dead of a coronary. What she had verbalized came true. She has now been widowed for more than twenty years. And she still cannot forgive herself.

Did her curse really cause his death? Highly doubtful. Did the fight and the hurtful words lead to the coronary? They may well have contributed. But what the wife kept repeating over and over again at the funeral and in the years since was the plaintive plea, "If only I would have known that was going to be his last day on earth. If only I would've known he was going to die."

How stupid the argument looks in retrospect. Had they only known those were going to be their last hours together, how differently would they have spoken to each other?

There is no greater grief, I learned in my many years in the rabbinate, than that of survivors of the death of their mate in the aftermath of a disagreement marked by disparaging words.

What is the correct response to "if only I had known he was going to die?" Perhaps it is simply, yes, of course, that is something you should have known because it is the fate that none of us can escape; it is no less than our human destiny.

The coffin and the *kittel*, the reminders of our mortality, could help us change the way we live our lives if only we took their message more seriously on a daily basis.

How remarkable that, even for a rabbi, it took the dramatic moment of my frightening diagnosis to make me fully appreciate this profound truth.

3

THE THREE WISHES

The day of death is concealed so that man may build and plant.
—Midrash Tanhuma

My diagnosis also led me to think about a fascinating question.

Accepting the reality of death, would you want to know beforehand when you are going to die?

What do you feel is the best way to go? Is your ideal the sudden and unplanned death taking you away without any premonition? Or would you want to have some warning, to have time to settle your affairs and to take care of unfinished business?

Would you wish for the gift of prophecy to let you in on the divine decision before it happens? Or do you agree with Jack Nicholson's classic line that "you can't handle the truth"?

True, we are hardly ever granted the choice.

Yet there is one biblical story in Jewish tradition that offers us the remarkable answer of one of the patriarchs. It comes from the Midrash, the classical rabbinic interpretations of the Torah, as part of a tale of three wishes by three very wise men. According to legend, God's acquiescence to their three requests changed human history forever.

The three men were Abraham, Isaac, and Jacob. Strangely enough, what each one of them asked for seems to be something the world holds in contempt.

The very first time the Bible makes reference to old age is with regard to Abraham. "And Abraham was old and well stricken in age; and the LORD had blessed Abraham in all things" (Genesis 24:1). Why had this never been mentioned previously in connection with anyone else? The rabbinic answer: because *this was the first time that noticeable aging had ever happened!*

Ask the youth-obsessed culture of our day to tell you what is good about old age, and the only thing most young people will be able to come up with is that, as Maurice Chevalier said, "It beats the alternative." The visible passage of time mocks our former strength and gives lie to our previous beauty. We "dye" to get rid of our white hairs and we masquerade in the garments of teenagers in a vain attempt to deny our years.

How remarkable then to learn that Abraham pleaded with God to bless him with the very sign we today consider a curse. Here are the words the Midrash put into the mouth of the founder of monotheism:

> Master of the universe, if there is no such thing as old age, a man and his son will enter a place and the people there will not know who deserves more honor. They will look the same. There would be no difference between an immature child and the mature man who has acquired a certain level of intelligence, experience and wisdom. That is not good. If you will be so kind, crown us with old age. Put a little white in the hair, make a person look a little bit older, more distinguished. Then others will be able to differentiate between them and know to whom to give greater respect.

The Midrash concludes that upon hearing this request, God said to Abraham: "A good thing have you asked for. And from you it shall begin." And that's why "Abraham was old and well stricken in age; and the LORD had blessed Abraham in all things."

Let me stress that what Abraham asked for were the benefits of aging. He didn't request nor receive its disabilities. He understood the benefits of white hairs and a wrinkled brow. He desired the signs that allow the world to recognize a person with experience and wisdom as someone precious and special in their midst. He knew that cultures that respect only the young prefer strength over knowledge, power over profundity. What Abraham brought to the world as a result of his wish being fulfilled was divine agreement with his desire that age be honored, as it deserves, for those ways in which it is superior to youth.

Isaac too had a wish. The Midrash implies it in the verse that tells us, "When Isaac grew old, his eyes became weak from seeing, and he became blind" (Genesis 27:1). Nowhere before in the Bible do we find any mention of physical affliction. It is a biblical first and seems to come out of nowhere. How can we account for his blindness? This too, remarkably enough, was the divine response to a prayer.

The Midrash fills in the blanks. "Master of the universe," Isaac said to God,

> if people were to die without having borne any affliction, they will arrive in the next world with a tremendous debt to pay. After all, nobody is perfect, and everyone will have to atone in some way for his or her sins and errors. I am afraid to face you, never having suffered hardship on this earth. I note too that the challenge of confronting difficulties as well as finding the faith to overcome them will make me a better person. I pray, therefore, let me take upon myself some suffering now, so it

will diminish the balance that I will surely have to pay later in the next world and make me more worthy.

To this request, God again replied, "A good thing you have asked for. And from you, it shall begin."

For almost all people, pain is something to be avoided at all cost, and disabilities are detested. Julius Caesar came to this conclusion: "It is easier to find men who will volunteer to die than to find those who are willing to endure pain with patience."

And yet there are those who come to understand that character, as Booker T. Washington put it, is the sum of all we struggle against. Helen Keller had the profound wisdom late in life to say, "I thank God for my handicaps, for, through them, I found myself, my work, and my God." Confucius taught it in his aphorism, "The gem cannot be polished without friction, nor man perfected without trials." And Isaac was the first one to intuitively grasp this truth and have the courage to plead for it to play a role in his life.

Surely the Midrash doesn't come to make a case for masochism. It isn't foolish enough to describe every infirmity as a heavenly gift, every disability as a divine blessing. That would be absurd. There is much about human suffering that we cannot understand or attempt to justify. But it is an important reminder for us that there are ways in which suffering may at times achieve such a noble purpose that those who are truly wise can voluntarily seek it.

Which brings us to Jacob, the third patriarch who made a wish that, on the surface, seems much more curse than blessing.

He too is described with a biblical first. Before him, there is no record of anyone whose death is preceded by a final illness. The almost universal legend has it that in the very earliest days, the way people died was with a sneeze. Man was created by way of God blowing His spirit into Adam's nostrils. The moment of death therefore saw the final breath of life expelled from the same place it had originally entered. To this day, a sneeze elicits a response of "Gezundheit," "God bless you," or any of the other hundreds of expressions in different languages that see the need to quickly offer a blessing for life and good health after what our subconscious cultural heritage identifies with death.

Jacob wasn't afraid of dying. What he deeply feared, however, was a sudden death, unexpected and without warning. He also turned to God with an appeal. "Master of the universe," he prayed, "people are dying without any advance indication. Their breath is taken from them, and they are gone in an instant. They sneeze and they are dead. They do not have a chance to settle their affairs, to make peace with those they have wronged, to ask forgiveness of God and fellow man. I want to know when I'm going to die—at least a few days before my parting. Please, God, give me the gift of a final illness before I am cut down by the Angel of Death."

For yet a third time, God replied, "A good thing you have asked for. And from you, it shall begin." So in Genesis 48:1, we first find the word for serious illness, *choleh*, in Hebrew. A messenger comes to Joseph to tell him, "Behold, your father is ill." Shortly thereafter, we learn that Jacob dies, but not before he has the opportunity to bid a final farewell to his family.

Imagine. Jacob could have departed from this world in the same way as all of his contemporaries. No worry, no stress, no anxiety. Not a death that includes the sad scene of family sitting close by, tearfully forced to come to terms with an imminent tragedy.

Yet Jacob chose the way of awareness.

Even though throughout his life he always recognized his mortality, he felt there was a great deal to be gained from the time that precedes a final parting.

I have witnessed many people making great use of their last moments. We speak of preparing to imminently meet our maker. It is an opportunity that by definition can come only once in a lifetime. According to the Talmud, sincere repentance at the very end can undo years of transgression. I've seen how the dying have become transformed as they reflect upon their past with the much clearer vision of approaching eternity.

Knowing that one is about to die permits reconciliations that otherwise would never have been possible. I have seen enemies embracing at a deathbed, children estranged from parents apologizing, husbands and wives in the midst of divorce proceedings begging each other for forgiveness.

In the case of Jacob, he had the opportunity to call all of his sons to his bedside and to tell them he wanted to bless them. Yet the blessings are odd in their phrasing. Jacob didn't say, "You should have a good life" or, "You should become very successful." Jacob's blessings actually were exhortations. They were instructions. In some cases, they were even critiques.

Why then, we might ask, were they called *blessings*? The answer is obvious. His criticisms were meant for their own good; they were all in their best interest. He was pointing out their character flaws only so that they might have a better understanding of their failings.

And why did he never do that earlier? The answer is obvious. *Were he not on his deathbed, his words would never have been accepted.* They would have simply been shrugged off as the complaints of an old man who just didn't understand. Worse yet, they might have been construed as insulting and might have caused a rift between him and his children.

But what people say right before death carries incredible weight.

A very wealthy man in my community who was not known for philanthropy, to put it mildly, suddenly endowed several major institutions with considerable gifts. I had occasion to ask him about the reason for his change of heart. He explained simply, "Because my mother, before she died, made a request of me. She begged me to help others with some of the great gifts God has bestowed on me—and I can't refuse to carry out her last wish."

A congregant who rarely made an appearance in the synagogue quite unexpectedly began to appear for services every Sabbath. A heartfelt talk with him explained the cause behind his spiritual awakening. "Rabbi," he said to me, "I know that I caused my parents a great deal of pain when I estranged myself from my religious identity. On his deathbed, my father said to me, 'The greatest gift you could give me after I die is to find your way back to the synagogue.' So showing up here every week is the least I can do for his memory."

Our day-to-day words can never have the same impact on others as those that are clearly our parting thoughts. They endow moments stamped as our last with very special meaning. It is surely easier to pass away in our sleep without any foreboding preliminaries. But Jacob knew why he wanted the gift of warning even though it came with suffering. His gain far exceeded his pain.

That must be of some comfort to all those who are granted time to prepare for their parting.

Like Jacob, they can be grateful for the special opportunity granted to them to say their final good-byes. And like Jacob, too, they can know that they have nothing to fear from what follows.

Which is why, after much thought, I now believe my diagnosis of death, with its message of warning, in its own strange way carries with it unspoken blessings.

4

THE FEAR OF DYING

The righteous has hope in his death.

—Proverbs 14:32

What is it that makes us so afraid of death?

We take many journeys in life where we know very little about our destination. But somehow death is different. Our most powerful fear is rooted in our inability to imagine our nonexistence.

Perhaps we will simply disappear without a trace. Perhaps we will no longer have any consciousness of our being. Perhaps to be dead means to be gone forever with the only remnant of our having existed confined to memories among the living.

We are afraid because we fear that nothing about us will matter anymore. We will be . . . simply nothing. And that is as frightening as it is unimaginable.

But what if the reality of death is totally different? What if death is not the end of life but the beginning of a new kind of existence? What if, as Johann Wolfgang von Goethe so beautifully put it, "Life is the childhood of our immortality?"

Long ago Socrates cautioned us that "to fear death is nothing other than to think oneself wise when one is not. For it is to think one knows what one does not know. No one knows whether death may not even turn out to be one of the greatest blessings of human beings. And yet people fear it as if they knew for certain it is the greatest evil."

It is almost impossible for us to think of our survival beyond the grave. The meaning of our selves is defined by our bodies. We spend our days on earth concerned with caring for our physical needs. How could we possibly continue to exist when what makes us who we are turns to dust?

Our minds are incapable of coming to grips with a changed perspective of this magnitude.

A remarkable Midrash (a rabbinic commentary from the time of the Talmud) offers us a way to begin to think about the possibility of life after death. It asks us to imagine the following scenario: Picture twins before birth resting peacefully in the womb of their mother. Their mouths closed, fed with no effort on their part through the tube entering their navels; warmed by the fluids of the embryonic sac, they feel completely at peace and secure. They can't possibly conceive of a more comfortable or different way of life.

Allow them now, if you will, the gift of consciousness. Assume that they are aware of their surroundings, and imagine that they begin to consider their future. They recognize changes taking place around them, feel themselves descending, and start to debate about what is going to happen to them.

The brothers each have strongly opposing views. One is by nature an optimist, the other a pessimist. The first is a believer, the second a skeptic. The believer is certain that another life awaits them after they are expelled from their present home. "I can't believe," he says with assurance, "that God would have put us here for nine months, cared for us, nurtured us, and allowed us to grow and develop without any purpose. There must be some greater plan that we still do not know. Our presence here could only have been preparation for a more glorious life to follow. It's impossible to think that all we can look forward to is total oblivion."

His brother, however, is much more of a realist. He despises wishful thinking and unsupportable expectations. For him, faith—as Marx would put it—is no more than "the opiate of the masses." "There you go," he says disdainfully to his twin, "confusing your hope with truth. The obvious fact is that everything that gives us life—the womb we live in, the cord from which we are fed, the security of our sac—is only here. Once we leave this place, we must die."

The believing brother again tries to make his case. He suggests that once out of the womb, they will be able to move even more freely. He talks about the possibility of other ways of getting food. He shares his dream of a kind of independence that goes beyond their present imagination. But unfortunately, he cannot put it into words. Lacking any contact as yet with life as it's lived on earth, he is stymied when his brother puts down his views as impossible and asks him to defend his ideas with concrete examples.

So the twins come ever closer to their destined meeting with birth, separated by drastically different opinions about their fate. The believer is confident he will not only survive but also be even better off than he was before. The skeptic morosely awaits the collapse of his world in the coming down of the final curtain.

Suddenly, the water inside the womb bursts. There is a pushing and pounding. The twins realize that they are being forced from their home. The traumatic moment is here. The believer is the first one to exit the wall. His twin brother, still inside, listens attentively for any clue from the other side. With grieving heart, he takes note of a piercing cry coming from his brother.

"So I was right after all," he tells himself. "I just heard my poor brother's scream of death." And at that very moment, a joyous mother and father are congratulating each other on the birth of their first child, who has just made his presence known by his cries of life.

What appears like death when viewed from one perspective is in reality a higher form of life. Death and rebirth are synonymous; one leads to the other.

How can we live outside of our bodies? How can we live outside of the womb? Both questions present levels of difficulty that seem equally unanswerable. Yet the miracle of birth enables us to rise to a higher level of being even without the seemingly life-giving support of the umbilical cord. So too, isn't it possible that what we call *death* is the way our souls have been granted the freedom to soar above the physical limitations of body and achieve a more blessed spiritual existence?

Elisabeth Kübler-Ross, who dedicated her life to studying death and the dying, wrote that in her many years of being present at the moment when life slipped away, what most moved her was the sight of the sudden serenity and peacefulness that invariably accompanied the passage from one state to another. She has chosen to describe death as "breaking out of a cocoon and emerging as a butterfly." Our bodies during life represent physical limitations. Without them, we are for the first time able to soar to heights previously unattainable.

The great inventor Thomas Edison, just moments before his death, emerged from a coma, opened his eyes, looked up, and said: "It's very beautiful over there."

The nineteenth-century Hasidic rabbi Mendel of Kotzk taught his disciples not to fear death by offering yet another parable. He told them, "Death is just a matter of going from one room to another—and the latter is far more beautiful."

I will never forget the incredible occasion when I had an opportunity to share these insights with a number of teenagers in a high school class I taught at my congregation. The topics we usually covered were meant to respond to the interests of the students. I encouraged questions and free-flowing discussions. One day the group decided to talk about that day's major headline, the death of a relatively young pop star who was an idol to most of them.

"We talk about God all the time and yet this seems so unfair," was the general consensus. How could their hero have died with such a glorious future still before him? Wasn't death the ultimate tragedy that challenges our belief in the goodness of God?

I wondered how best to explain to them that the apparent cruelty of death didn't necessarily negate faith in a loving Creator. And so I told them the story of the as-yet-unborn twins in the womb debating their destiny. I asked them to open their minds to the possibility of a world after this one. I explained that this was the view of Jewish tradition and urged them to consider its ramifications.

Suppose, I said to them by way of a comparison that suddenly entered my mind, we were at this moment having a great party. Picture it as an event like no other that you have ever attended. All of us are enjoying ourselves immensely when there is an unexpected knock on the door. We greet the uninvited guest, who announces that one of them, whom for the purpose of illustration I called Paul, must come with him immediately and leave the party.

We all feel bad. Poor Paul, we say. He's having such a fantastic time, and now he has to go. What is it we have to know, I ask my students, before we can decide whether this impromptu invitation to leave us warrants our sadness? The students are quick to answer. Of course we have to first know the reason for the messenger's mission. Is it to tell him something bad has happened to a member of his family and rush him to a hospital? Or is it perhaps to take him to a bigger and better party—to a surprise birthday bash, for example, planned by friends who at this very moment are waiting for him to appear so that they can shower him with gifts and with love?

The students understood my analogy. We can never define enforced parting as depressing until we fully understand its purpose. True, we would have a right to feel sad for ourselves, for now missing Paul's presence. But we ought to feel compensated for our lack by the knowledge that Paul was fortunate enough to go somewhere even better.

It was time for the class to be over. I expected the students to rush out as they normally did after our session. But this time, one of the young girls chose to linger. She approached my desk and said, "Rabbi, can I ask you to do me a favor?" "Of course," I responded before even knowing what she wanted. "Rabbi," she told me, "what you just explained to us literally gave me goose bumps. It just spoke to me in ways I can't really describe. I've never heard anything so beautiful and so moving. Could you do me a favor and repeat it for me just one more time so I can take notes and get down every word. I just want to memorize it."

And so, to the best of my ability, I repeated the lecture to the young girl whose name, by seeming coincidence, was Paula—the female equivalent of the name *Paul* I had randomly chosen for my illustration.

For the second time, Paula devoured every word I uttered. When I finished, Paula said, "I just know that everything you told me is true. And Rabbi, I have to thank you, because now I'm sure I will never ever be afraid of dying."

Paula left with a huge smile. Little did I know then that would be the last time I would ever see her.

The very next day, Paula decided to walk from our town of Oceanside, Long Island, to visit a friend in Long Beach. On the way, a car driven by someone on drugs veered off the road and struck Paula, immediately killing her.

I had the daunting task of delivering a eulogy for a beautiful sixteen-year-old who would never grow to adulthood, never marry and bear children of her own, never fulfill her potential.

What could I possibly say? And so I told the story of what happened at the very last class of Hebrew high school that she attended. I shared with the mourners what had seemed inexplicable to me at the time—Paula's almost obsessive interest in the subject of death, a subject so far removed from the usual concerns of a teenager.

What made Paula so intrigued with the meaning of death? Is it conceivable that on some subconscious level, it was a premonition of what would happen to her on the next day? There's no way I will ever know, but intuitively I believe it is possible.

What gave me great solace, as I know it did to her friends and family, was the knowledge that before Paula passed away much before her time, she had the opportunity to reflect upon death and to conclude that there is more to life than what we experience here on earth.

These ideas that I shared with my class are certainly reassuring. But how do we know they are true?

For that we will turn to the forthcoming chapters.

5

THE TESTIMONY OF WITNESSES

The LORD kills and makes alive,
He brings down to the grave, and brings up.

—I Samuel 2:6

For thousands of years, humankind has struggled with the mystery of death without benefit of personal testimony from any of its victims.

No matter how much we want to pierce the veil of secrecy that blocks our view of the beyond, we recognize our human limitations. Death is always a one-way trip that doesn't allow for a return visit to earth to reveal its secrets to the living.

What happens when we die? Even if we accept the idea of survival in another form after our bodies cease to function, we are stymied by the lack of any scientific evidence simply because the dead cannot speak.

Or so we thought.

But in the last half century, something dramatically new has been added to the equation. There are those who still dismiss it as unverifiable. Yet it is slowly gaining ground even among those who've never identified themselves as particularly religious or spiritual.

Our secular age is coming to terms with belief in some kind of survival after death because of the countless cases of testimony from people who died and were brought back to life.

Many movies in the past, including two films at the 2017 Sundance Film Festival, explored the theme of the afterlife: *The Discovery*, starring Robert Redford, wondering, what if the existence of the afterlife was scientifically proven? and *A Ghost Story*, with Ben Affleck dealing with past life regrets and loves. And from the not-so-distant past, who doesn't remember the closing scene from one of the highest grossing movies of all time, *Titanic*, when the dying heroine is greeted on the other side by people who have died before her?

The Good Place, a successful American comedy television series on NBC, focuses on a woman who wakes up in the afterlife and is introduced by Michael (Ted Danson) to "The Good Place," a Heaven-like utopia he designed, in reward for her righteous life.

Books with the very same theme have consistently gone to the top of bestseller lists. Who would have believed that works like James Van Praagh's *Talking to Heaven* or Brian Weiss's *Many Lives, Many Masters* would sell many millions of copies and change cultural perceptions of the afterlife around the world? Mitch Albom's *The Five People You Meet in Heaven,* a parable about life after death where the hero in heaven sequentially meets five pivotal figures from his life, was on the top of the *New York Times* bestseller list for over two years. And, heralded in the *Newsweek* magazine cover story of October 8, 2012, was the remarkable story told by Dr. Eben Alexander, a neurosurgeon with impeccable academic credentials, in his international and autobiographical bestseller *Proof of Heaven: A Neurosurgeon's Journey into the Afterlife*.

In the words of Raymond Moody, one of the most prominent authorities in the field of life after life:

> I am confident that Dr. Alexander's story will capture world-wide interest. It will inspire many to accept that there really is life after death. I suspect his book will be a global game-changer. It has seismic implications and may help humanity arrive at a more accurate understanding of life's true meaning and purpose in the larger sense. Dr. Eben Alexander's near-death experience stands as perhaps one of the crown jewels of all near-death experiences. The knowledge of what he experienced raises the bar for serious investigators and pundits. It marks the beginning of a new era of rational investigation of humankind's deepest mystery, life after death.

What accounts for this contemporary obsession with an idea formerly relegated to the realm of religion or disparaged as mystical nonsense? What prompted the secular world to suddenly be so receptive to the concept of an immortal soul?

The answer almost assuredly lies in an incredible medical breakthrough in the 1970s that began to play a significant role in the lives of thousands of people. Until then, death was truly the great unknown. Shakespeare's observation in *Hamlet* seemed to express a truth that would remain valid for all time: "Death is the undiscovered country . . . from whose bourne no traveler returns." There was no way we could ever test what was taught to us by faith. That a conscious soul survives after death had about as much rational support as the claims of a medium at a séance.

And then, thanks to increasingly sophisticated resuscitation techniques, people died—and then returned to tell us what it was like!

Professionals who have done groundbreaking work in the field, such as doctors Elisabeth Kübler-Ross and Raymond Moody, have come up with the name NDE—near-death experience—to describe the phenomenon. But NDE survivors were really far more than just "near" to dying. They were for all intents and purposes dead and then brought back to life.

We may argue—and many have—that anyone now alive by definition didn't really die. But what allows us to think of those who have gone through this experience as having been closer to "the other side" than to what we call *life* is the fact that they were *clinically dead*. Their brains didn't show even a flicker of activity. Their hearts had stopped beating. There was no way for sensations to register, for sights to be recorded, and for sounds to be heard. And yet these people were able to "recall" what happened in the rooms in which their bodies rested, to describe who came and went after they heard themselves pronounced dead, and even to repeat conversations that took place in the presence of their "dead" bodies in minute and accurate detail.

With which part of their nonfunctioning brains did they remember, and how could they possibly see and hear? Their physical bodies were no longer capable of performing these tasks. Small wonder that almost everyone who went through an NDE experience, whether they initially were believers, die-hard skeptics, agnostics, or atheists, came to an unshakable belief in the existence of a nonphysical soul that survives the death of the body.

That is exactly what convinced Dr. Alexander after a transcendental near-death experience in which he was driven to the brink of death and spent a week deep in a coma from an inexplicable brain infection. As he recounts it, he spent seven days in a coma caused by a rare case of *E. coli* bacterial meningitis. During his week in the ICU, he was present "in body alone," since the bacterial assault had left him with an "all-but-destroyed brain." He notes that by conventional scientific understanding, "If you don't have a working brain, you can't be conscious," and a key point of his argument for the reality of the realms he claims to have visited is that his memories could not have been hallucinations since he didn't possess a brain capable of creating even a hallucinatory conscious experience.

While his body lay in a coma, Dr. Alexander journeyed beyond this world and was guided into the deepest realms of super-physical existence. Before he underwent his journey, he would have dismissed similar descriptions as the stuff of fantasy. He would never have been able to reconcile his knowledge of neuroscience with any belief in heaven, God, or the soul. Today Alexander is a doctor who believes that true health can be achieved only when we realize that God and the soul are real and that death is not the end of personal existence but only a transition.

As someone whose views were dramatically changed by personal experience despite their going counter to all of his previous medical training, Dr. Alexander pointedly challenges us to welcome views formerly rejected as unsubstantiated theology into the realm of scientific possibility. That's why he urges us to understand that beneath the "religion versus science" debates that lead nowhere, there is another deeper, and fantastically more fruitful, discussion going on, sparked by a new group of participants— people who have undergone near-death experiences, out-of-body experiences, and other experiences suggestive of the survival of consciousness. They are increasingly being allowed to describe the experiences they've undergone. And a small but select group of scientists has decided to take them seriously, to ponder, with the combination of fierce intellectual rigor and vigorous, empirical open-mindedness that all good science demands, what they might mean.

In this debate, Dr. Alexander stresses, we are allowed to stay open—as all true science must—to what kind of universe we really live in. When a person who has been clinically dead returns to life and describes traveling to other, larger worlds, we need to listen to what this person says and ask, not whether what they say sounds silly to us (truly new discoveries nearly always do), but whether there might be some truth to it. We must overcome our innate tendency to deny and disbelieve, just as people in Europe had to do in the great age of exploration, when travelers returned with tales of lands and peoples and ways of life entirely beyond the ken of those who had sent those explorers out to begin with.

Indeed, doctors as well as hospitals are of necessity taking note. When I delivered a talk on this subject at a conference of doctors in Houston, Texas, the staff shared with me a remarkable new rule put into place for surgeons performing life-threatening operations. There had been a number of occasions when doctors succeeded in bringing someone back after all signs of life were gone, only to be castigated by the patient. "How could you have been kibitzing with each other and making jokes when my life hung in the balance?" they would ask, able to repeat almost entire conversations word for word from those who had stood around their bed when by scientific measurements they were "dead."

By all accounts, this was medically impossible. Yet the facts outweighed logical assumptions. Even when the brain no longer functioned, there was something indefinable that was able to record and to remember. And these "memories" often reflected unfavorably on what should have been the serious demeanor of doctors. So the new hospital rule was that no one was to say anything that might in the smallest way be considered objectionable, even if the patient was clinically dead—apparently giving the lie to the old saying that "dead men tell no tales."

Theologians find it ironic that the medical profession has inadvertently succeeded where countless generations of religious leaders previously failed. Modern medicine has at last given us some quite convincing evidence for the existence of the human soul.

The very technology designed to keep the body alive at all costs has revealed that the body is secondary to a higher meaning of self.

Human beings are more than bodies. We have nonphysical, invisible aspects of reality that outlive our mortal "containers."

At last we have come to understand what is almost certainly meant by the Bible when it tells us that we are created "in the image of God." God is immortal; our souls, sharing His divine essence, must surely share the gift of immortality.

And if we remain unconvinced by the anecdotal evidence of NDE, let us turn to the Bible to see what we can glean from divine wisdom in our quest to explore the end of our journey here on earth.

6

THE SILENCE OF THE BIBLE

The secret things belong unto the LORD our God . . .
—Deuteronomy 29:28

A good portion of the world agrees with Patrick Henry that "the Bible is a book worth more than all the other books ever printed."

For people of faith, it is supposed to have all the answers.

Yet, strangely enough, a response to the questions surrounding death seems to elude us. Is there more to the story of our biblical threescore and ten? Are we doomed to total extinction after our short stay on earth? Is there life after this one, and if there is, what is it like? Will we meet our loved ones again in another world, and will we recognize each other? Will we still have personal awareness and consciousness, and will we know who we were and who we are? Will we ever be able to communicate with the living? Is there a heaven and a hell—and what happens in the former to make it so wonderful and in the latter to be so feared?

The questions are limited only by our imagination. The answers span the gamut from a denial of any form of survival after death to a belief in our continued existence replete with physical earthly pleasures—like seventy-two virgins—for the devout.

Surely a book written by God, or at the very least inspired by Him, should offer the answers.

Remarkably, and sad to say, it doesn't—at least not clearly, other than by way of hints that might be said to imply hidden meanings.

Scholars are intrigued by this omission. For some, that serves as proof that the concept of an afterlife is an idea unknown to the Bible. Its very omission speaks against its validity.

But Judaism, as well as most other mainstream religions, accepts both the Bible as truth, and life after death as a certainty. In *The Encyclopedia of Religion* (vol. 6, pg. 506), Roger Lipsey writes, "Very nearly all traditions speak of the mortal body and of a potentially undying presence within it."

The belief in the existence of the soul and its immortality goes back many millennia; it was central to the religions of the Egyptians, the Sumerians, and almost all of the cultures with which biblical Israel came into contact. Without a doubt, the idea was known to all, and its acceptance was apparently self-evident.

So why is it so hidden in the Bible?

Professor of Bible Herbert Chanan Brichto offers the fascinating insight that the afterlife was not mentioned in the Bible *precisely because it was a given*. It didn't need to be said. Everyone already knew *that*. The Bible was meant to teach us how to improve our earthly status, how to live life to the fullest, how to conduct ourselves in a way that would be pleasing to the Creator.

Traditional commentators have been less troubled by the seeming omission of such a major concept. That's because in Jewish thought there has always been the idea of an orally transmitted Torah that accompanied the written word. Words are subject to misinterpretation. They require further clarification, explanation, and elucidation. That's why God wasn't content to simply hand over a book; He made sure to teach its true meaning to Moses so that through the oral tradition, the correct and full import of every text would be preserved.

The oral law, the explanations of Biblical verses, that accompanied the text in every generation it was taught to, consistently incorporated the idea of an afterlife into our proper understanding of the written word.

Mystics make even stronger claims for their understanding of "the other world." Kabbalah, the transmitted wisdom of esoteric ideas too profound for the average person, asserts that this information was passed down for millennia to a select few in every generation from the time of Creation.

But this raises the question: If it is something we ought to know, why wasn't it communicated clearly? Why should the written Torah permit belief in an afterlife to be questioned by allowing it to make its appearance only in the oral tradition? And why should secrets of the beyond be granted to only the select few who achieve mastery of the mystical Kabbalah and its teachings?

Let me share with you a personal story that can shed some light on this issue. It was one of those moments I will treasure for a lifetime.

The year was 1956. I had just been ordained and felt I needed a vacation after completing years of rigorous study. Together with two other newly minted rabbis, we decided on a trip that in those days was considered rather exotic. We chose pre-Castro Cuba as our destination—not too far away, not too costly, beautiful, and totally different from our New York City environment.

One day as we rode through Havana and its outskirts, our taxi driver/guide pointed out a magnificent estate and told us that this was the residence of the world-famous writer Ernest Hemingway. "Stop the car," we told him. "We want to go in." He shook his head and vehemently told us, "No, no, that is impossible. No one can just come in to visit. Only very important people who have an appointment."

With the chutzpah of the young, I insisted that we would be able to get in and approached the guard with these words: "Would you please call Mr. Hemingway and tell him that three rabbis from New York are here to see him."

How could Hemingway not be intrigued? Surely he would wonder what in the world three rabbis wanted to talk to him about. Perhaps he would see us as material for a future story or novel. And so we held our breath. And the guard himself could not believe it when the message came back from the house that Mr. Hemingway would see us.

We were ushered into Hemingway's presence as he sat with his wife, Mary, in their spacious den. What followed, we subsequently learned, was a verbal volley meant to establish whether it was worthwhile for him to spend any time talking to us. He questioned us about our backgrounds, threw some literary allusions at us to see if we would understand their meaning, asked what we thought was the symbolic meaning of some passages in his *A Farewell To Arms*—and then after about fifteen minutes, totally changed his demeanor and spoke to us with a great deal of warmth and friendship.

"Rabbis," he said to us, "forgive me for having been brusque with you at first but before continuing I had to make certain it was worth my while to talk to you. To be honest, I've long wanted to engage a rabbi in conversation. I just never had the opportunity—and now suddenly out of the blue you've come to me."

Hemingway then opened up to us in a most remarkable manner. He told us that for many years he had a great interest in religion, which he pursued privately and never discussed or wrote about. He said that during one period of his life, he set aside time to study many of the major religions in depth. On a few occasions, he even attempted to personally follow the rituals of certain faiths for a short time to see if they would "speak to him."

I'm basically not a spiritual person, he confessed. But he said that after he thought deeply about the different religions he studied, he came to an important conclusion. Fundamentally, he realized all religions fall into one of two major categories. There are religions of death, and there are religions of life. Religions of death are the ones whose primary emphasis is preparation for an afterlife. This world and its pleasures are renounced in favor of dedicating oneself totally to the world to come. Obviously, he added, that isn't for me. What he respects, he continued, are religions like Judaism, which stress our obligations to what we are here for now on earth rather than in the hereafter.

With his perceptive mind, he summed up the essence of Judaism perhaps better than most Jews themselves can. Judaism is a religion of life. "Choose life," says the Bible many times. Death of course is recorded, but what happens afterward purposely remains hidden from the reader.

I took the opportunity then to compliment Hemingway on his analysis and had the temerity to ask if I might teach him something that would add to his insight. I told him of the biblical law that prohibits the Kohanim, all the members of the Jewish priesthood, from coming into any contact with the dead. If they did so, they would be considered impure. To this day Kohanim, descendants of Aaron, cannot enter a funeral chapel while there is a body inside.

The rabbinic commentators questioned the reason behind this law. The answer that resonates most with scholars is that the Torah wanted to ensure that the priestly class, those assigned to dedicate themselves to the spiritual needs of their people, did not misconstrue their primary function. In too many religions, the holy men devote themselves almost exclusively to matters revolving around death. Even in our own times, the only connection many people have with a spiritual leader is at a funeral. That is why the Bible forbade the priests from having any contact with the dead—so that they spend their time, their efforts, their concerns, and their energy with the living.

And then Hemingway smiled and thanked me for sharing with him this beautiful idea. I still don't think it gets any better than this, to be the recipient of gratitude from a world-renowned Nobel Prize winner.

My encounter with Hemingway became all the more poignant when on July 2, 1961, I learned that the man whose hand wrote the books we revere to this day chose to use it to put the barrel of his shotgun into his mouth and to purposely take his own life. Somehow he was never able to find a spiritual source to lean on to give him a reason for living. He had taught the world, in his words, "But man is not made for defeat. A man can be destroyed but not defeated." And yet, tragically, the biblical ideal to "choose life" that he praised in our meeting could not guide him in the end.

Yet his insight into the fundamental difference between religions is today more relevant than ever. Osama bin Laden is dead, but his words aptly describe the contemporary clash between two major spiritual orientations. Islamic fundamentalism stands opposed to Western civilization. Bin Laden starkly defined the difference between the two: "You Americans worship life; we worship death."

To worship death is to teach children from early youth that their greatest achievement is to die the death of a martyr. To worship life, on the other hand, is to teach children that the best way to make their lives meaningful is to live up to their potential so that, through their achievements, they leave the world a better place for mankind to survive and prosper.

Judaism directs us to reject the idolization of death. God has entrusted us with too many responsibilities while we are alive to forsake it.

Which brings us back to our original question: the Bible's silence about the world to come. The Torah was given at a time when the religions of the Hebrews' neighbors were preoccupied almost entirely with death. The Egypt from which the ancient Hebrews fled was a nation that devoted its efforts and much of its wealth to preparations for the afterlife.

Death in Egypt of old was viewed, not as an ending, but the beginning of a journey to eternity. Embalming preserved the corpse by extracting the organs, filling the shell with salt and linen, and wrapping it in bandages and amulets. The next life, ancient Egyptians believed, would be an enhancement of this one. The dead would need to be sustained and amused, so their tombs were filled with food and drink, instructive texts, games, and jewelry. Model figures, called Shabti, were also buried with the dead between the Middle Kingdom (3,500–4,000 years ago) and the Ptolemaic Period (2,300 years ago). They provided friendship for the deceased and acted as their laborers. Slaves were put to death and entombed together with their masters so that they might continue to serve them. The Egyptians also believed that if the pharaoh's body could be mummified after death, the pharaoh would live forever—and that's why they built the pyramids as tombs designed to protect the buried pharaoh's body and his belongings.

It was to the Hebrews of this time that a new way of life, rather than a way of death, was presented. The Bible didn't need to teach those who received it that the soul survives after death. Their world was populated by people who excessively devoted their lives to death, at the cost of properly living life. What they needed to hear was how to reverse these priorities.

To wean them away from the cultures of Thanatos worship, the Bible spoke solely in terms of terrestrial obligations. Love your neighbor, not death, as yourself. Free the slave; do not inter him with the wealthy so that he may continue to serve his master in the afterworld. Help the widow; do not just tell her to rejoice because her husband is now in a better place. Be kind to your worker; do not force him to labor with backbreaking effort in order to build pyramids for the greater glory of the deceased.

King Solomon put it well in his book of Proverbs. "It [the Torah] is *a tree of life* unto those who grasp hold of it" (Proverbs 3:18).

The Torah's omission of details about death and its aftermath may well have been a purposeful decision by God to help us focus on our human obligations on earth—while allowing us to be pleasantly surprised after leaving it.

7

WHAT THE BIBLE DOES TELL US

And the dust returns to the earth as it was, and the spirit returns unto God who gave it.

—Ecclesiastes 7:12

But the Bible's silence about death isn't the whole story.

The Bible includes tantalizing clues about immortality. The learned and pious able to decipher them could be trusted not to worship death over life, even with the knowledge that the soul survives its earthly journey.

For the masters of Kabbalah, a hint for this idea found expression in the very first Hebrew letter of the Torah. In English, the opening verse of the Bible is of course, "In the beginning God created the heavens and the earth." In Hebrew, the first word is *B'reishit*—in the beginning—and the first letter is the *second* letter of the Hebrew alphabet, the letter known as *bet*. (It's interesting to note that the very word *alphabet* comprises the names of the first two letters in Hebrew, *aleph* and *bet*).

The mystics have a tradition that there's a message hidden in the fact that *aleph,* even though it enjoys top billing in the alphabet, wasn't selected to open God's book describing creation. The reason is that Hebrew letters also serve as numbers. *Aleph* is *one*, *bet* is *two*, and so on. The very first idea implicit in the story of the creation of the world is that *God in reality created not one world but two*—the world we live in from the womb to the tomb and the world reserved for our souls in a purely spiritual form of existence after our passing.

And there is more that Kabbalah tells us is concealed in the first letter by way of its shape. According to tradition, in every Torah text, be it the one handwritten by a scribe, from which Jews read in the synagogue, or all of our printed versions from which we study, the first letter, *bet,* must be written large, twice the size of its neighbor. Obviously that is meant to draw special attention to it.

And what are we to learn from it? Here is what the letter looks like in Hebrew: בָ

Hebrew reads from right to left. Looked at from that direction, the letter is closed on both the top and the bottom as well as on its right side. It only has one "opening," closed off from what precedes but exposed to the words that follow. Mystically, it is God telling us that although much will be revealed in this book, what is above us in the heavens and below us in the nether regions, as well as everything that came before our creation, is to remain sealed, closed-off details denied to human beings.

The two commentaries, the first teaching us that there is a world in addition to ours and the second emphasizing its inaccessibility, serve as a perfect illustration of the concept that can best be described as "reveal and conceal." On the one hand, the shape of the letter tells us that *we won't be told* that there are secrets meant to be inaccessible to us. On the other hand, the existence of another world is alluded to by the numerical message of the letter to indicate that, if we are smart enough to understand it, there was a dual creation and our present world is only half the story.

Farfetched? Only if you consider these interpretations as products of human ingenuity introduced by later readers and far removed from the original intent of the Author. However, if it is true, as the Kabbalists claim, that these are insights always transmitted concurrent with the text itself and an integral part of their deeper meaning, they offer a fascinating glimpse into a far more profound understanding of God's word.

Even secrets aren't meant to be hidden forever. The concealed is permitted to become revealed to those wise enough to grasp the truth.

If these allusions to another world are too esoteric, we can reveal a much stronger clue to the Bible's position on human immortality from the creation of Adam.

> And God created man in His own image, in the image of God created He him; male and female created He them (Genesis 1:27). Then the LORD God formed man of the dust of the ground, and breathed into his nostrils the breath of life; and man became a living soul. (Genesis 2:7)

We've already introduced the idea in the previous chapter: to be in God's image is obviously not a reference to physical resemblance. God is not man, nor is He subject to the weaknesses and frailty of flesh. To be like God is to share with Him part of His essence. That is our soul. And the part that is godly within us maintains its godly characteristic of immortality. More, the Almighty breathed into Adam's nostrils the breath of life. The breath that entered carried within it man's soul as well as its divine source.

Everything has a powerful drive at some point to return to its source. The physical part of man, the body, came from "the dust of the earth." When it can no longer function, it disintegrates and becomes reabsorbed into the ground from which it was originally taken. Our "image of God" aspect, however, was a direct gift from above. God blew into Adam of His spirit. When that spirit can no longer fulfill its sacred mission because it has lost its bodily dwelling, it too wants nothing more than to return to its source. And so the soul ascends back to God.

We speak of someone who died as having expired. The word, by way of its Latin root, means "to have expelled air." *Spirit* comes from the word for breath. The English language maintains a link to the biblical story of human creation. The infusion of God's *spirit,* the divine breath that endows us with a soul, is what gives us life. When that leaves us, we become a mere corpse, a container without content, the "dust of the earth" without the presence of the portion of the Almighty that granted us the dignity of our humanity. To expire is to expel the breath of our creator. That is what we call death: the separation of the soul from our body, each one destined to return to its original source.

An intelligent reading of the biblical text leads us to the recognition of an immortal aspect of our being. This isn't reading *into* a text but rather *reading out of* it what logic suggests, even for those who do not have an oral tradition confirming it.

I hope I'm clear in all of this that I don't mean to convince nonbelievers. I merely suggest that the idea of a soul that is godly, that survives after our death and that represents the most profound part of our identity, is something that should readily find a place in our understanding of biblical thought. It appears just a layer beneath the surface, even though the Bible doesn't dwell on it, for the reasons we've already discussed.

In fact, there is one phrase repeated ten times in different forms in the Pentateuch, that for many scholars is even clearer, and undeniably a reference to another world after death—a world whose inhabitants not only live on forever but also maintain awareness of their past identity. In describing the deaths of Abraham, Isaac, Ishmael, Jacob, Aaron, and Moses, the Torah uses the phrase "and he was gathered to his people." When it appears with regard to Abraham, it clearly isn't a poetic metaphor for death or another way to tell us he was buried. The phrase is sandwiched between these two facts and would be totally redundant: "And Abraham expired, and *died* in a good old age, an old man, and full of years; and *was gathered to his people.* And Isaac and Ishmael his sons *buried* him in the cave of Machpelah, in the field of Ephron the son of Zohar the Hittite, which is before Mamre" (Genesis 25:8–9).

In each of the instances where the phrase is used, the intent seems to be to tell us that immediately following death, these righteous people were reunited with their ancestors who predeceased them. Simply put, death is defined as "reunion with the past, a meeting of souls who share incorporeality."

I've noted, before, the observation of Elisabeth Kübler-Ross that the moment of death seems to bring with it a peaceful and almost joyous serenity. Part of the explanation for this may be found in a remarkable mystical commentary on a passage in the book of Exodus. Moses is recorded as pleading with God to allow him to "see" the Almighty. "Show me, I pray thee, Your glory" (Exodus 33:18). God tells him that this is impossible. "You cannot see my face, for no man can see My face and live" (33:20). The statement might just as well have concluded with the words "no man can see My face." What is added by the caveat "and live"? The implication is that *while we are alive* we are not permitted a clear vision of God. But at the moment of death, when we prepare to enter a new kind of existence, we *are* granted the ability to "see" the Divine.

Perhaps that is the meaning of the remarkable story Mona Simpson, sister of Steve Jobs, revealed in her eulogy for her famous brother. When she arrived at his deathbed, she recounted, she found Jobs surrounded by his family. "He looked into his children's eyes as if he couldn't unlock his gaze"—and managed to hang on to consciousness. "He looked," she said, "like someone whose luggage was already strapped onto the vehicle, who was already on the beginning of his journey, even as he was sorry, truly deeply sorry, to be leaving us. However, he began to deteriorate. His breathing changed. It became severe, deliberate, purposeful. I could feel him counting his steps again, pushing farther than before. This is what I learned: he was working at this, too. Death didn't happen to Steve, he achieved it."

After making it through one final night, Simpson said, her brother began to slip away. "His breath indicated an arduous journey, some steep path, altitude. He seemed to be climbing. But with that will, that work ethic, that strength, there was also sweet Steve's capacity for wonderment, the artist's belief in the ideal, the still more beautiful 'later.'

"Steve's final words were monosyllables, repeated three times. Before embarking, he'd looked at his sister Patty, then for a long time at his children, then at his life's partner, Laurene, and then over their shoulders past them.

"Steve's final words were: 'Oh wow. Oh wow. Oh wow.'"

The man who in all probability was the greatest visionary of our generation had one last revelation. It apparently overwhelmed him with its beauty. He could only respond to it with a three-times-repeated exclamation of amazement.

What was it that he saw? Jewish tradition teaches that our last moment on earth grants us a glimpse of the Almighty!

As we will later describe, the most common occurrence recorded by those who went through an NDE event was to see what they could only explain as a powerful, warm, and healing light that they had never before witnessed. They were overwhelmed by its brightness and the spiritual goodness that seemed to emanate from it. "Man cannot see Me and live" are the words of the Bible. "Man *will* see Me at death" is the unstated implication.

Jewish law demands that immediately after death, we shut the eyes of the departed. It is a custom that is almost universal, found in countless cultures. The reason remains obscure to most scholars, but Jewish mystics attribute it to this idea: when the soul leaves the body, the person enjoys a heavenly vision that is so holy that the eyes should no longer be exposed to any other sights.

Until now, all of our biblical examples may still appear debatable. There is one story in the Bible, however, that indisputably demonstrates not only survival of the soul after death but the more significant reality—that it can at times even communicate with the living. It doesn't appear in the five books of Moses, which abide by the principle of maintaining the secrets of the afterlife, but comes from one of the books of the Prophets, traditionally accepted as part of the holy Bible.

In the book of Samuel 1, chapter 28, we find a remarkable story about King Saul, terrified by the advancing Philistine armies and desperate for divine guidance from the prophet Samuel, who by this time was already deceased. The king, we are told, consulted with a woman known as "the witch of Endor," who was renowned for her ability to communicate with the departed:

> And the woman said unto him, "Behold, you know what Saul has done, how he has cut off those who have familiar spirits and the wizards out of the land. Why then do you lay a snare for my life, to cause me to die?"
>
> And Saul swore to her by the LORD, saying, "As the LORD lives, there shall no punishment happen to you for this thing."
>
> Then said the woman, "Whom shall I bring up unto you?" And he said, "Bring me up Samuel."

. . . And Saul perceived that it was Samuel, and he stooped with his face to the ground and bowed himself. And Samuel said to Saul, "Why hast thou disquieted me, to bring me up?" And Saul answered, "I am sore distressed; for the Philistines make war against me, and God has departed from me and answers me no more, neither by prophets nor by dreams. Therefore I have called you, that you may make known unto me what I shall do."

Then said Samuel, "Why then do you ask of me, seeing the LORD has departed from you and has become your enemy? . . . For the LORD hath rent the kingdom out of your hand and given it to your neighbor, even to David.

"Because you obeyed not the voice of the LORD nor executed His fierce wrath upon Amalek, therefore has the LORD done this thing unto you this day. Moreover the LORD will also deliver Israel with you into the hand of the Philistines; and tomorrow shall you and your sons be with me. The LORD also shall deliver the host of Israel into the hand of the Philistines."

The woman was in fact able to communicate with the dead. The Bible itself verifies what took place. It was the no-longer-alive Samuel whose spirit appeared, angrily asking, "Why did you disturb me by bringing me up?" The conversation between King Saul and the spirit of Samuel concludes with the prophet informing the king that he would be defeated by the Philistines and that he and his sons would die in battle on the very next day.

These predictions come true. Samuel's spirit is brought back from the dead to tell the king what will happen and, more importantly, why. There isn't the slightest suggestion in the Bible that what took place is impossible or fictitious—there isn't even any surprise at the fact that the dead are still "alive" and can communicate with the living.

True, the story presents difficulties in terms of biblical law. There is a prohibition against necromancy, the act of calling on the dead for guidance. We might well have assumed that the law is based on a Torah view that necromancy is fraudulent, and its practitioners to be avoided because they are assuredly quacks. But that seems to be disproved by the story of Samuel. The true reason necromancy is a sin is that it moves us away from God and His guidance, not because its premise is false. We are meant to turn to the Almighty and not human spirits, but that doesn't take away from the reality of their existence.

The Talmud does in fact record numerous instances when the spirits of the dead sent messages to the living. In my own experience as well, on two separate occasions, I've heard directly from people whose stories confirm this, and I have no reason to doubt the veracity of what they shared with me.

One of my congregants, during World War II, was a bombardier on a military aircraft. While looking out the window as he drew near to an enemy fighter plane, he suddenly heard the clear voice of his departed father shouting out his name. He turned around to see where the voice was coming from. At that very moment, bullets passed through the precise spot he was at before turning. The call that made him move saved his life. The voice was that of his father, who had died seven years earlier.

This incident was not only life saving but also life changing. From that day on, the man adopted a totally different spiritual attitude toward life. Today he believes with certainty in an afterlife, and he has no fear about his own eventual passing.

The second story concerns another congregant who miraculously survived the Holocaust. He lived in a small village in Hungary. One night he was sleeping, he told me, when he found himself having a recurring dream. His mother, who had died years before, appeared to him and told him he must leave this town immediately. He turned to and fro, tried to sleep again, only to be reprimanded by his mother's voice, which insisted that he leave immediately and hide out in the woods. The dream was so vivid that he felt he had to act. He left his house and his town, only later to learn that on the very next day, the Nazis had come in and slaughtered every resident. He still cannot understand how he had the conviction to be guided by a dream. To this day, he is convinced that it was really his mother's spirit that spoke to him and enabled him to survive.

The obvious question people always ask whenever I recount these stories is, "Well, why then isn't everyone whose parents are gone beneficiaries of the same kinds of warnings? Why don't the spirits of those who love us intercede more often to guide us in times of distress?"

It is something I cannot answer. Obviously, the lines of communication between the living and the dead are normally closed. What challenges us, and what we cannot explain, is why at certain times and for certain people the lines are allowed to be opened. But the very fact that on rare occasions, as infrequent as they may be, there *can* be a temporary "crossing over" of the dead speaks louder than their silence as proof of their survival.

It is both helpful and necessary to remember the famous words of William James: "If you wish to upset the law that all crows are black, you mustn't seek to show that all crows are black; it is enough if you prove one single crow to be white."

From my own experience as well as from countless similar stories shared with me by colleagues, I have absolute certainty that many "white crows" of interaction between the dead and the living are carried on constantly—even though I cannot account for the "black crows" who opt for silence rather than dialogue with their living loved ones.

Our survey of the Bible is almost complete, with only one final and major point to be made. Implicit in God's entire book is the assurance that He is fair and just. "For all His ways are justice; a God of faithfulness and without iniquity, just and right is He" (Deuteronomy 32:4). Those who follow Him and live a life in accord with His values will be blessed; those who disregard Him will be punished. This promise is repeated as a recurring mantra throughout the Torah. And yet life seems to contradict this fundamental religious principle!

It is not only Job who was perplexed by the problem of why the righteous suffer. It is all of us who can't help but realize that very often life's rewards aren't apportioned to the pious, nor divine punishments meted out to the wicked. Life is unfair. One has to be blind not to see it. How could we then possibly reconcile reality with biblical promises?

It is a theological problem that can have only one answer. The rewards and punishments we witness during the span of our lifetime don't tell the whole story. If they did, the Bible would be a lie, deluding us with a distorted picture of the consequences of our actions.

Can the wicked really get away with it forever? Can the righteous be deprived for all time of the rewards they so richly deserve? We have a right to demand justice from God, just as Abraham did when he told the Almighty, "Far be it from you; shall not the judge of all the Earth do justly?" (Genesis 18:25). The Torah declares itself to be a Torah of truth. The only way to resolve the problem of life's unfairness is to posit another world in which the scales of reward and punishment are finally righted.

We have no choice but to conclude that the survival of the soul after death and its judgment must be assumed if we are to accept the Bible's validity.

8

THE TUNNEL OF LOVE

This world is comparable to the antechamber before the World to Come. Prepare yourself in the antechamber, so that you may enter the banquet hall.

—Talmud, Ethics of The Fathers, 4:16

"God is in the details," goes the famous saying.

If we agree there is an afterlife, we'd love to know more about it.

To find out, we have two principal sources available to us. The first is the testimony of the NDE group who "have been there," if we are to take their accounts at face value. The second is a tradition of many centuries passed down in the esoteric knowledge of Kabbalah—knowledge originally meant to be kept secret from the masses.

Allow me to make something clear: I identify the second source of this information as *Kabbalah* only because I am a rabbi, and this, after intensive study, is what is familiar to me. What I have learned from my research, however, is that most of the Kabbalistic concepts about life after death are also found in countless other sources—the *Tibetan Book of the Dead*, the Qur'an, as well as the

holy books from the mystics of a host of other cultures and religions. They are apparently universal ideas that have somehow been
transmitted to all seekers of truth, no matter their particular religious orientation. As eternal truths, they transcend different religious practices.

And what is more than amazing, in comparing the reports from
NDE survivors and the revelations of Kabbalah, we see that *there
is almost not a single discrepancy between the two.* There are by
now tens of thousands of recorded interviews with people who
were "brought back to life," and with minor variations, they all
incorporate the same basic themes.

This to me is perhaps the most interesting aspect of all near-
death experiences: their universal similarity. Without reference to
religion, race, social status, age, or the value system of the individ-
uals involved, those who were pronounced clinically dead found
themselves going through most, if not all, of the stages Raymond
Moody summarized in his groundbreaking work, *Life after Life*,
with this composite vignette:

> A man is dying, and as he reaches the point of greatest physical
> distress, he hears himself pronounced dead by his doctor. He
> begins to hear an uncomfortable noise, a loud ringing or buzz-
> ing, and at the same time feels himself moving very rapidly
> through a long, dark tunnel. After this, he suddenly finds him-
> self outside his own physical body, but still in the immediate
> physical environment, and he sees his own body from a dis-
> tance, as though he is a spectator. He watches the resuscitation
> attempt from this unusual vantage point and is in a state of
> emotional upheaval.
>
> After a while he collects himself and becomes more accus-
> tomed to his odd condition. He notices that he still has a body,
> but one of a very different nature and with very different pow-
> ers from the physical body he has left behind. Soon other

things begin to happen. Others come to meet and to help him. He glimpses the spirits of relatives and friends who have already died, and a loving, warm spirit of a kind he has never encountered before—a being of light—appears before him. This being asks him a question, nonverbally, to make him evaluate his life and helps him along by showing him a panoramic instantaneous playback of the major events of his life. At some point he finds himself approaching some sort of barrier or border, apparently representing the limit between earthly life and the next life.

Yet he finds that he must go back to the earth, that the time for his death has not yet come. At this point he resists, for by now he is taken up with his experience in the afterlife and does not want to return. He is overwhelmed by intense feelings of joy, love and peace. Despite his attitude, though, he somehow reunites with his physical body and lives.

Later he tries to tell others but he has trouble doing so. In the first place, he can find no human words adequate to describe these unearthly episodes. He also finds that others scoff, so he stops telling other people. Still, the experience affects his life profoundly, especially his views about death and its relationship to life.

Not one of the people who have shared this experience, upon returning to life, is ever again afraid of death.

As an aside, Moody added an interesting postscript. Becoming known for his interest in the subject, Moody was often asked to lecture about his findings. Invariably, not during the question-and-answer period but at some later point as he mingled with the audience over refreshments, at least one person would come over to him to whisper that "the stages" Moody outlined actually happened to him or to her.

There are two points of interest I believe we can derive from this. The first is how it confirms the obvious frequency of this experience—with the advances in modern medicine, it seems that a near-death experience is far from a rarity. The second is even more interesting. Why is it that *none of these people who admitted to Moody that they could substantiate what he said from personal experience chose to speak up publicly*? They would explain to Moody that they were hesitant to speak up in the lecture hall because they feared being labeled odd, delusional, or even crazy. Confessing to a spiritual encounter beyond human comprehension frightened them. They chose silence over sharing what they knew to be true to prevent being laughed at.

I have personally tested this phenomenon in my own lectures as well. Whenever I've discussed this subject with a group of at least one hundred listeners, at least one person has approached me afterward to privately share the same testimony. The one occasion I thought would prove to be an exception to the rule was when I had an opportunity to address six hundred teenagers in a camp setting. The theme was the concept of the soul, and although the essence of talk wasn't about death—too depressing for these youngsters—I did spend a few moments describing how NDE pointed to proof of the soul's existence. Surely, I said to myself, among a group so young, I wouldn't have anyone approaching me afterward with a personal story of resuscitation from death. Yet I had not one but two teenagers who—again privately—told me their stories, each one involving an automobile accident, when they "died"; saw themselves out of body; witnessed as if from a distance all that was happening; could describe people and conversations around their body; felt themselves falling through a long tunnel at the end of which was a spectacular light, only to be suddenly stopped, even though at this point they wanted to continue on; and were told they had more to accomplish in life and commanded to return.

THE TUNNEL OF LOVE

The description of events after death always includes the awareness of a journey, most often a passage through a long tunnel. Both the Talmud and the Kabbalah make reference to this stage of the dying process. During this trip, the person is aware of a review of his or her entire life coupled with strong feelings of judgment, both by oneself and by others.

It's interesting to note that Plato, the classical Greek philosopher of the fourth century BCE, already had occasion to record an aspect of this phenomenon. In *The Republic*, he writes about a soldier who reported a near-death experience:

> Er, the son of Armenious, by race a Pamphylian once upon a time was slain in battle, and when the corpses were taken up on the tenth day already decayed, he was found intact, and having been brought home, at the moment of his funeral, on the twelfth day as he lay upon the pyre, revived, and after coming to life related what, he said, he had seen in the world beyond. He said that when his soul went forth from his body he journeyed with a great company and that they came to a mysterious region where there were two openings side by side in the Earth, and above and over against them in the heaven two others, and that judges were sitting between these, and that after every judgment they bade the righteous journey to the right and upward through the heaven with tokens attached to them in front of the judgment passed upon them, and the unjust to take the road to the left and downward, they too wearing behind signs of all that had befallen them, and that when he himself drew near they told him that he must be the messenger to humanity to tell them of that other world, and they charged him to give ear and to observe everything in the place. (Rep. X, 614 b, c, d)

What is missing in this account is the tunnel, a feature that usually is given great prominence in contemporary recollections of the near-death experience. Yet it is striking that more than two thousand years ago, a philosopher known for his total commitment to truth included this unverifiable story in his major work, not only as possible but also as a probable description of reality.

Perhaps the tunnel made its way into Plato's work by way of his famous allegory of the cave in *The Republic*. The account of the soldier, Er, of a "mysterious region" may have been the source for his collective cosmology, the key to the difference between the perceptions of two different kinds of reality. In the allegory, there is a vision of universal light, immortal soul, reward and punishment, reincarnation, and even tunnels, all strong allusions to a near-death experience. In a profound sense, the allegory highlights the human error of mistaking what we see as ultimate reality, when in fact we perceive only the shadows—the same insight that separates the understanding attained by the soul after it is freed from its earthly constraint.

Plato records Socrates as teaching his students to imagine a scenario in which what people take to be real would in fact be an illusion. He asks Glaucon to imagine a cave inhabited by prisoners who have been chained and held immobile since childhood; not only are their arms and legs held in place, but their heads are also fixed, compelled to gaze at a wall in front of them. Behind the prisoners is an enormous fire, and between the fire and the prisoners is a raised walkway, along which people walk carrying items on their heads "including figures of men and animals made of wood, stone and other materials." The prisoners watch the shadows cast by the men, not knowing they are shadows. There are also echoes off the wall from the noise produced from the walkway.

Socrates suggests the prisoners would take the shadows to be real objects and the echoes to be real sounds, not just reflections of reality, since they are all they had ever seen or heard. They would praise as clever whoever could best guess which shadow would come next, as someone who understood the nature of the world, and the whole of their society would depend on the shadows on the wall.

Socrates then supposes that a prisoner is freed, climbs out of the cave with dazzled eyes, and discovers the blazing sun and the true world that it floods with light:

> When one was freed from his fetters and compelled to stand up suddenly and turn his head around and walk and to lift up his eyes to the light, and in doing all this felt pain and, because of the dazzle and glitter of the light, was unable to discern the objects whose shadows he formerly saw, what do you suppose would be his answer if someone told him that what he had seen before was all a cheat and an illusion, but that now, being nearer to reality and turned toward more real things, he saw more truly? (Rep. VII, 515 c, d)
>
> After some time on the surface, however, the freed prisoner would acclimatize. He would see more and more things around him, until he could look upon the Sun. He would understand that the Sun is the "source of the seasons and the years, and is the steward of all things in the visible place, and is in a certain way the cause of all those things he and his companions had been seeing." (516 b–c)

On one level, the allegory conveys the soul's philosophical awakening. On another, it has remarkable parallels to NDE reports: the shock of discovering through the light the truths that previously had been hidden; the radical shift in consciousness; the journey from a world that was no more than shadows to one that allows clear and truthful vision. What Socrates saw as the ultimate goal achieved by a mind philosophically searching may be the very gift granted to all of us when we leave the cave of shadows that we call "life."

In that sense, the path through which we are transported after death to allow us celestial vision may well be the best example of a tunnel of love.

It is a path charted by philosophers, described by Jewish tradition, explored by mystics of all major faiths, and experienced by those granted an opportunity for added life, who returned to share with us their vision. Should we not acknowledge its existence even before we find ourselves on the road not *yet* taken?

9

KNOWING THE UNKNOWABLE

Into thine hand I commit my spirit: thou hast redeemed me, O
LORD God of truth.

—Psalms 31:5

Yet we still cannot help but wonder.

Can the stories that come from NDE survivors be taken literally? Or are they simply a delusion that is a side effect of the process of dying?

Critics of NDE testimony discredit their tales as illusions triggered by the stress of approaching death or claim that these are hallucinations produced by chemical changes in the dying brain. They claim that what happens is actually a biological response. They say that some of the reported characteristics may be caused by oxygen starvation affecting the brain and producing hallucinations. The feeling of complete serenity is due to the release of endorphins. The "tunnel" effect might be explained as an ophthalmological phenomenon known as "form constants," images produced by the actions of the visual nervous system independently of signals received by the retina, due to stress. Other researchers have written that the tunnel experience is due to increased levels of carbon dioxide in the blood. Carl Sagan, noted Cornell University scientist and astronomer, theorized that the tunnel experience is a left-over memory of the birth experience.

Yet many of these alternate explanations do not hold up to ordinary scientific standards. In his important work, *Recollections of Death: A Medical Investigation*, Dr. Michael Sabon, an Atlanta cardiologist, records how he measured the blood levels of patients experiencing an NDE and found their blood oxygen levels to be normal. Carl Becker, a philosophy professor from Southern Illinois University, examined pediatric research and concluded that babies don't remember being born and don't have the facilities to retain the experience. Dr. Sam Parnia, of the University of Southampton (England), reported that one-tenth of his patients surviving cardiac arrest stated having NDEs. None of these patients exhibited brain-wave activity during this period. He ruled out hallucinations, since their descriptions were too realistic in detail. Their brains were not capable of such clear processes, nor would they be able to recall memories under such conditions.

In his book *Consciousness beyond Life*, Dr. Pim van Lommel, a world-renowned cardiologist practicing in The Netherlands, dismisses the oxygen-deprivation theory based on the fact that it is "accompanied by an enhanced and lucid consciousness with memories and because it can also be experienced under circumstances such as an imminent traffic accident or a depression, neither of which involves oxygen deficiency."

Van Lommel also dismisses the theory that the tunnel effect experienced in many NDEs results from a disruption of oxygen to the eye or the cerebral cortex. He points out that oxygen deficiency in these areas cannot explain meeting deceased relatives in the tunnel, as has often been reported, or hearing beautiful music. He explains why carbon dioxide overload, various chemicals, and other physiological theories do not account for the NDE. "When new ideas do not fit the generally accepted (materialist) paradigm, many scientists perceive them as a threat," van Lommel writes. "It is hardly surprising therefore that when empirical studies reveal new phenomena or facts that are inconsistent with the prevailing scientific paradigm, they are usually denied, suppressed, or even ridiculed."

Having grown up in an academic environment, van Lommel was of a materialist/reductionist mind-set before he began studying the NDE and the nature of consciousness. He has closely examined all the arguments made by the scientific fundamentalists and now has a more positive outlook. "That death is the end used to be my own belief," he states with conviction. "But after many years of critical research into the stories of the NDErs, and after a careful exploration of current knowledge about brain function, consciousness, and some basic principles of quantum physics, my views have undergone a complete transformation. As a doctor and researcher, I found the most significant finding to be the conclusion of one NDEr: 'Dead turned out to be not dead.' I now see the continuity of our consciousness after the death of our physical body as a very real possibility."

It's understandable that scientists are very hesitant to accept truths that are scientifically unverifiable. Anecdotal evidence fails the test of being able to be replicated. But scientists also bring their own biases and prejudices to the table. As paleontologist Stephen Jay Gould correctly reminded us, "Facts do not speak for themselves; they are read in the light of theory."

Sir Fred Hoyle, the distinguished English astronomer and mathematician, put it this way in his influential work *Highlights in Astronomy*:

> Writers on scientific method usually tell us that scientific discoveries are made "inferentially," that is to say, from putting

together many facts. But this is far from being correct. The facts by themselves are never sufficient to lead unequivocally to the really profound discoveries. Facts are always analyzed in terms of the prejudices of the investigator. The prejudices are of a deep kind relating to our views on how the universe must be constructed. (pp. 35–36)

The scientific mind-set is biased toward rejecting any hypothesis that isn't grounded in proof beyond doubt, a mind-set that makes it equally impossible to determine conclusively the existence of God and our fate after we die. When areas of knowledge are unknowable to us because of our human limitations, scientists will tend automatically to say *no* while those with more open minds will say *maybe*.

To scientists who scoff at NDE testimony, it might be appropriate to recall the words of Arthur Schopenhauer: "All truth passes through three stages: First it is ridiculed. Second, it is violently opposed. Third, it is accepted as being self-evident."

Scientific objections deserve to be taken seriously. But in the interest of truth, scientists equally have an obligation to take seriously the one unimpeachable part of near-death experiences: *Those who return have knowledge they could not possibly have acquired in any scientifically accepted or understood way.*

Dr. Melvin Morse, a Seattle pediatrician, did extensive work with children who suffered cardiac arrest and survived. In his bestselling works *Closer to the Light* and *Parting Visions*, he convincingly concluded that their near-death experiences weren't drug induced, the psychological product of fear, or culturally conditioned. He described the case of one nine-year-old patient, Kate, who was resuscitated after drowning. When she revived, she described physical details of the hospital scene while she was unconscious. She told how a guide took her through a tunnel where she met her deceased grandfather. When a figure of light appeared and asked if she wanted to go back to her mother, she responded affirmatively, and the next thing she knew, she woke up in her hospital bed.

Now here, to my mind, is the most fascinating part of all: Kate added matter-of-factly that during her NDE, she traveled out of body to her home. There she saw her brother playing with a G.I. Joe in a Jeep and her sister playing with a Barbie doll. She described the clothes her parents were wearing, where her father sat in the living room, and what her mother was cooking.

Every one of her observations was confirmed.

Scientists can't simply dismiss evidence of paranormal wisdom. Without a convincing alternative explanation, Kate could only have known these things because her soul did indeed travel out of body to her home.

And this ability to know the unknowable is echoed in countless NDE records.

One of the striking aspects shared by people who had NDEs is their meeting with previously departed relatives or close friends who come to greet them. This spiritual "welcome wagon" is always and exclusively composed of those who are no longer alive. We might suppose that if this were a mere hallucination, at least some of the affected would visualize living people nearest and dearest to them—a parent, a child, or a lover. *That never happened.* All the NDEs reported that they were met by people already deceased.

Amazingly, it turns out that among those who greeted them were often people who had very recently passed away without their knowledge.

Those they came to greet didn't know of their deaths and yet they were part of "the committee" leading them through the tunnel on their final journey.

Granted, all of these accounts are anecdotal. Scientists still remains skeptical. Yet, there are three very strong points that are highly convincing:

- People who have experienced NDE know things they could not have learned any other way.
- They have a clear memory of meeting with deceased relatives and friends—even when they were previously unaware that these people had died.
- These near-death experiences are all strikingly similar.

NDE doubters never seem to feel they have an obligation to deal with these convincing proofs. Without an alternative explanation, don't we have sufficient reason to accept the most likely interpretation—that their accounts are true?

Why do we persist in denying the spiritual? Clearly the facts speak more pro than con for the existence of an afterlife.

Dr. Morse writes that his research convinced him that by dying, we become "more alive, more fulfilled and blissfully happy." He is sure he will get the chance someday himself to verify what one little girl said to him after her near-death experience: "Heaven's fun. You'll see!"

The *American Journal of Diseases of Children*, a prestigious mainstream medical journal, published Morse's early findings in 1986. At that time, many leading physicians expressed their reservations. The medical profession was not yet prepared to say "Amen" to an explanation of death that owes more to God than to Galen. But it's surely noteworthy to recognize that, even in the medical community, acceptance of the idea of the soul and its survival after death has made more progress in the last few decades than in all the preceding millennia.

More recently, research on near-death experiences has come from several academic disciplines, including the fields of medicine, psychology, and psychiatry. Interest in this area of study was originally spurred by the work of such pioneers as Jess Weiss, Elisabeth Kübler-Ross, George Ritchie, and Raymond Moody. This was soon followed by the establishment of the International Association for Near-Death Studies (IANDS) in 1981. IANDS is an international organization that continues to encourage scientific research and education on the physical, psychological, social, and spiritual nature and ramifications of near-death experiences. Among its publications are the peer-reviewed *Journal of Near-Death Studies* and the quarterly newsletter *Vital Signs*.

Among the scientific and academic journals that have published, or are regularly publishing, new research on the subject of NDEs are the *Journal of Near-Death Studies*, the *Journal of Nervous and Mental Disease*, the *British Journal of Psychology*, the *American Journal of Diseases of Children*, *Resuscitation*, *The Lancet*, *Death Studies*, and the *Journal of Advanced Nursing*.

At long last, scientists are beginning to take a new look at a universal experience reported by lucid people from around the world—rejected solely because it failed to meet the rigorous standards of proof required by the scientific community. Peter Fenwick, a neuropsychiatrist and fellow of the Royal College of Psychiatrists in the UK and emeritus senior lecturer at the Institute of Psychiatry in London, with over two hundred published papers on brain function, has conducted extensive research into end-of-life phenomena. He put his finger, I believe, on the reason why scientists are so reluctant to give any credence to NDE or inexplicable areas of knowledge most often dismissed as spiritual or religious.

He writes:

> The reductionist scientific culture of the West is almost alone in its unshakable belief in the finality of death. The slowly progressing scientific dominance of a materialist view has led us to abandon the concept of the transcendent. It is argued that consciousness is formed entirely by the brain. The idea of the journey after death has almost completely disappeared from the scientific perspective and we are left with a random universe where dying is simply a mechanical process. However, recent studies of the mental states of the dying suggest that this is too limited a view. I am a neuropsychiatrist, which means that I've been trained in the understanding of the brain and its functioning as well as in the nature of the mind. So I stand in the zone between mind and brain. I have studied the dying process and written scientific papers in peer reviewed journals to disseminate a new view of what actually happens when we die, and to ask what the experiences of the dying could contribute to our understanding of consciousness. (Leslie Kean, *Surviving Death*, 2017, p. 134)

We can only look forward with great anticipation to the day when modern medicine will know as much about the aftermath of death as it does about the time that precedes it. Perhaps then science and ancient spiritual wisdom will be viewed as worthy partners in humanity's pursuit of eternal truths.

10

MISSION *NOT* ACCOMPLISHED

The purpose of man's life is not happiness but worthiness.

—Felix Adler

Near-death experiences share another characteristic: they all speak of journeys aborted.

If death was their destination, we must wonder why the NDErs never completed the process. Why did they return to the land of the living?

Invariably, those who have experienced the trip tell us the reason: Much as they were tempted to go forward to the brilliant light at the end of the tunnel, they heard the decree to go back *because their mission in life was not yet accomplished.*

Of all the things death may have to teach life, this perhaps is the most important.

It powerfully reminds us that the miracle of life has a purpose. Our presence on earth is part of a divine plan in which every one of us is given a crucial role to play.

In this light, the admonition of Horace Mann assumes a much more profound significance. "Be ashamed to die until you have won some victory for humanity," he wrote. It is not simply because we ought to feel that a life that isn't lived well is wasted. Far more, it represents the failure to complete a divinely ordained mission.

This is a profound reason for us to reflect upon what happens after death while we're still alive. Perhaps it's best summarized in the following famous parable in traditional Jewish lore. A very wealthy man not known for his piety stood in a long line of those waiting to have their lives assessed by the heavenly court. He listened attentively as those who were being judged before him recounted both their spiritual failings and achievements. A number of them seemed to have the scales weighted against them until they suddenly remembered acts of charity they had performed, which dramatically tipped the scales in their favor. The rich man took it all in and smiled to himself.

When it was his turn, he confidently said, "I may have committed many sins during my lifetime, but I realize now the power of charity and good works can override them. I am a very wealthy man and I will be happy to write out a very large check to whatever worthy cause you recommend."

To which the court replied, "We are truly sorry, but here we do not accept checks—only receipts."

The true tragedy of death is that it represents the closing curtain on our ability to do any more good deeds. It is only what we bring to that moment that can earn us a legacy of achievements. Death ends the story of our response to our life's divine mission.

Those who are sent back to life after a near-death experience are very conscious of their responsibility to make their remaining years have significance. Be it through their careers, their relationships with others, or their responsibility for parents and children, they realize they have been spared for a reason and that the way they conduct themselves must justify their continued presence on earth. If only all of us would share the same sentiment!

What we can learn from NDEs is that every one of us is meant to achieve something related to our own potential. To embrace it is to validate our existence; to deny it is to deserve leaving life.

Sometimes the death of a young person who lived a life of righteousness can be explained with this concept. The Talmud records the story of the student of a prominent rabbi who was deeply depressed because his best friend perished in his early twenties. He couldn't contain his bewilderment and pleaded with the rabbi to help him understand God's ways. "My friend already accomplished so much in his short life. Why would God choose to take him away from us?"

The rabbi told his student to walk with him, and as they approached a farm, the rabbi said, "Look at that very strange sight before us. It is hardly noon and yet there is that farmer already leaving his field and going home." The student was perplexed. Why didn't the rabbi answer his question? Why was his attention diverted by a seemingly unrelated event? "Rabbi," he dared to ask, "what does this have to do with the question I asked you? And what is so strange about the farmer's actions—he finished his work and he is going home."

The rabbi responded, "May your ears hear what your own mouth has said. He finished his work and he is going home. So too when we conclude our designated task on earth the Lord lovingly calls us back to Him."

Those who die premature deaths that appear to our minds totally unwarranted may be receiving an early reward rather than an unjust punishment. They were placed on earth with a specific mission that, once accomplished, permits them to gain entrance to a better, more joyful world.

The converse of this story is that death may be the result of a divine decision that this person's failure to pursue his specific mission makes clear he's lost the right to remain on earth. We are given countless chances to work on our appointed task. God is patient. He waits for us to discover what it is, strewing many hints along the way. The clue to our unique role is implicit in our talents and distinctive characteristics.

Rabbi Yisrael Salanter, the famous nineteenth-century founder of the Jewish self-improvement program known as the Mussar movement, used to say that it is tragic for a person not to know his weaknesses, but it is doubly tragic if a person does not know his strengths. It is our strengths, our unique talents, that define our distinctiveness and clarify why God felt it necessary to place us here on earth. They are the keys to our divine service and the justification for our continued presence in the world. We are as different from one another as snowflakes, even when we appear to be alike. No one else who ever lived or will live was meant to do the task we were assigned.

Just as we need to view our talents as gifts from God to enable us to fulfill our unique mission, we have to recognize that our passions, those activities that give us a feeling of pleasure and fulfillment, are also given to us by God. The world's greatest cellist, Yo-Yo Ma, remembers that as a child he began playing the violin. He recalls that he felt no love for the violin, and was at best mediocre. Only when he took up the cello did his musical gifts fully manifest themselves. Passion identified his purpose; his purpose made him excel. Fulfilling his mission not only gave his life meaning but granted him life itself.

The NDErs grasp the specific task that warrants their return. It may be a child who still needs to be reared, a parent who requires the special care only this person can give them, or a mate who cannot manage on their own. In all these cases, those who have "come back from the dead" live their lives with far greater purpose and meaning. What they know for sure is that they had to return because their job wasn't finished.

Gilles Bédard's tunnel experience is a good illustration. The doctors at Sacré-Coeur hospital in Cartierville, Quebec, just north of Montreal, did not expect Gilles Bédard to live. Ravaged by a severe intestinal disorder for nearly five months, the nineteen-year-old, five-foot-eight-inch Bédard weighed just seventy-five pounds on November 17, 1973, when he developed a 105-degree fever and lapsed into a coma. A priest administered last rites, and Bédard's parents were at his bedside. But he recovered, and in the months that followed, he had vivid recollections of his glimpse of what he calls an "afterlife." Now living in Montreal, Bédard told deputy chief researcher Sharon Doyle Driedger that the experience had affected his life profoundly, leading him to his present career as a producer of New Age music, whose knowledge and expertise, combined with the thoroughness of his research, have made him Canada's New Age music specialist and one of the genre's most active proponents on the international scene.

> In the blink of an eye, my vision expanded and I went into a place like a cosmos where there were 12 people standing in a half-circle. They were all pure white lights and they had no faces. Beyond them was a tunnel. I wasn't afraid. I somehow knew these people although they weren't family or people I could recognize. It was as if they were waiting for me. I asked them what was happening, and they told me, "You are not going to die. You are going back to Earth. You have something to do." I asked them what it was, and as soon as I asked, it was as if I knew the answer. (http://www.near-death.com/resour ces/music.html)

Most of us do not have the benefit of a near-death experience and its lessons. But what we ought to take from them is that we too can only justify our lives by way of our own missions. We aren't sent back to the living; we're already here. But we are only here for the same reason: fulfilling our mission is the rent we have to pay to allow us to continue staying in our earthly abode.

Some years ago, I had the privilege of speaking at a retreat for the Gathering of Titans. They are a group of approximately one hundred CEOs of major corporations who get together annually at the Massachusetts Institute of Technology to refresh themselves intellectually and spiritually. For the printed program, every one of them was asked to succinctly summarize the philosophy, aims, and goals of their business by way of their mission statement.

Mission statements are a fact of life for every successful company. They define what the company hopes to accomplish, how it believes it will succeed, what its ultimate plans are for the future—what they hope to look like in 10, 20, and 50 years hence.

I suggested to these titans of industry that they consider writing a mission statement for themselves, for their personal lives, just as they did for their businesses. It would allow them to think about the way they define success and to measure their progress as they try to balance finances and family.

One of the most successful businesses of all time is certainly the search engine Google. Here is the way its cofounders summarized their objectives:

- "We have a mantra: don't be evil, which is to do the best things we know how for our users, for our customers, for everyone. So I think if we were known for that, it would be a wonderful thing."—Larry Page
- "The ultimate search engine would basically understand everything in the world, and it would always give you the right thing. And we're a long, long ways from that."—Larry Page

- "As we go forward, I hope we're going to continue to use technology to make really big differences in how people live and work."—Sergey Brin
- "Obviously everyone wants to be successful, but I want to be looked back on as being very innovative, very trusted and ethical and ultimately making a big difference in the world."—Sergey Brin

Imagine if we had similar clarity about personal goals and how we plan to achieve them. Imagine if we took our personal mission statement as seriously as a business manifesto. Imagine if we took the time to decide why God put us here on earth and then went ahead and fulfilled our life's purpose.

And how else can we discover exactly what our mission is?

I've mentioned divine hints. Let me add another.

King David writes, "The steps of man are directed by God" (Psalms 37:23). The Baal Shem Tov, the eighteenth-century founder of the Hassidic movement, explained this verse in the following manner: Although we go about our daily tasks at what seems to be our own initiative and will, our steps are "guided" for a spiritual and loftier purpose. We end up in a specific place so that we will have the opportunity to do what needs to be done from a divine perspective.

What this means is that we don't have to worry about *finding* our mission. God leads us to the location where our mission lies. He orchestrates the circumstances to ensure that we have the position and tools to fulfill it. The challenge is to seize the moment. When we find ourselves in a specific place and situation that speaks to our abilities and calls for our involvement, it is the greatest indication that there is something for us to accomplish there.

There is one thing we have to be very careful about as we try to determine the life task assigned to us. *We can't allow it to be the goals others have convinced us to pursue.* The world tries to seduce us to spend our lives acquiring wealth and possessions. Its slogan is, "He who dies with the most toys wins." But that isn't why we were put here on earth; that's why our material goods immediately abandon us at our passing. Einstein is surely wise enough to be relied on for his advice: "Try not to become a man of success, rather try to become a man of value."

Those who are mindful of the idea of mission take special notice of unexpected moments. A flight is rerouted, and you suddenly find yourself in a foreign place. You unexpectedly meet people who share their problems with you. You're forced to relocate for the sake of your career, and you abruptly discover new friends who need you. If we learn to view life from the perspective that nothing is merely coincidence and that, as the saying goes, "Coincidence is merely God's way of choosing to remain anonymous," we'll find spiritual clues scattered among our daily activities.

The most unforeseeable and unexpected events are the ones that very often have the greatest meaning. They are the directional signals for our souls. The more we turn away from the worship of material objects and concentrate on affirming our values, the closer we come to fulfilling the mission that identifies the meaning of our lives.

In Hassidic tradition, there is a beautiful parable that reminds us of how easily we can lose our way. Here is the story:

> Once there was a struggling merchant who heard of a land filled with diamonds and rubies, there for the taking. Nervous, hopeful, unsure of what he would find, he embarks on the journey and when he arrives is amazed to see: it's all *true.*
>
> On the ground, there are diamonds in place of sand and rubies instead of grass. Shyly at first, but then with increasing vigor, the man begins to gather gems. He fills one pant pocket, then the other, and just as he begins to stuff his suitcase full

of jewels, a few people gather round; it's their turn to be amazed.

For you see, in this land diamonds and rubies were so prevalent, that they weren't worth anything. No one could understand why this odd stranger would want them.

It wasn't long before the man realized that what he truly needed to buy food, or clothes, or to find a place to sleep, was . . . pebbles.

Our protagonist is disappointed but he's also a quick study. He starts several businesses and in a few years' time he becomes prosperous. You could in fact say that he becomes loaded—in pebbles.

Happy and sure of his success, the merchant is eager to reunite with his loved ones. He sends word of his return and sails home with all his assets.

Pulling into his home port, he looks around excitedly, spotting his family and friends. "I'm rich," he screams, beaming from ear to ear—until he notices their shocked expressions as they mull over what to do with a boatload of small rocks!

The story doesn't end there, however. It's been a long journey and a disappointing day once the man realizes that all the riches that he brought home have no value in his homeland. Deciding to get some sleep, he slips out of his clothing, and a small ruby or two falls out of his pocket.

These rubies were so precious in his native land that the man was truly rich beyond his wildest dreams.

As you might imagine, this story is a parable. Our souls come to this world to amass a "boatload" of good deeds (like a child's star chart on the fridge). Sadly, we all too soon get distracted and wind up chasing . . . pebbles. Thankfully, the good news is that no soul can traverse our world without picking up at least a few good deeds along the way—gems that can enrich our eventual worth from a divine perspective and make the entire trip more than worth its while.

And the gem that has the most value of all? The one that's labeled our own personal mission.

11

THE FATE OF THE BODY

Respect the body as the receptacle, messenger and instrument of the spirit.

—Samson Raphael Hirsch

As I write this, I have coincidentally just come back from a funeral. But, as I've told you before, I don't believe in coincidences. So I know that it was meant for me to write this chapter now.

I confess that ever since I received my frightening diagnosis, when I officiate at funerals, I look at the proceedings in a totally different way. I know that the remains of a person I knew well are in a confining box. I am there when the body is lowered into the ground and hear the clatter of earth as it is shoveled on the casket. And I can no longer fully distance myself from what I witness.

That, someday, is going to be me.

What does it feel like for someone who is as claustrophobic as I am? Like a child before a painful procedure, I wonder, does it hurt?

And then I push these fears out of my mind. They are merely emotional reactions to something that seems to be happening, but really isn't. Every one of those who have gone through near-death experiences confirms that the very first thing they were aware of was being outside of their body. They were immediately free of any pain, even if moments before they were in excruciating agony. They saw their own bodies from above, and although it seemed disorienting, they realized they weren't in it. Their body was no longer "them."

Religion, Kabbalah, and NDEs are in agreement: Death is the moment when the soul separates from the body. The former survives; the latter begins its movement to decay and dissolution.

We should not confuse the corpse with the person.

A fascinating story that occurred over two centuries ago highlights the legal significance of this concept according to Jewish law. In the city of Warsaw, two Jews who for many years had been the closest of friends became bitter enemies after a violent disagreement. In anger, both of them vowed, "I never want to see you again." For years, they kept their promise. They never attended the same parties, they never prayed in the same synagogue. They made certain never to be anywhere the other might be present.

As happens to all men, one of them died. The survivor began to reconsider how foolish their hatred was and how wrong it was for them to have ended their friendship. How could he atone for his sin, he wondered. And then an idea struck him. The greatest tribute someone could pay to another is to assist in preparing the body of the deceased for burial. And so, as a sign of his remorse and his willingness to repent for the years of his enmity, he asked for permission to join the Chevra Kadisha, the group involved in the holy work of tending to the body before interment, for his former friend.

Of course, there was one major problem. What about his oath? He had sworn to God to never see the man again. By participating in the washing of the body and the required dressing in funereal garb, he would of necessity "see" him. On the other hand, one might argue that seeing him only as a body was not truly to see the person and would not constitute a violation of his sacred promise.

The question was brought to rabbinic scholars, who debated the matter for hours. They attempted to resolve the difficulty with citations from a host of different Talmudic sources. They found it difficult to find an exact analogy in previous cases from which to draw a definitive conclusion.

A bystander, a simple Jew, far from a scholar, asked if he might offer his opinion. "I don't see the difficulty of the question," he meekly said.

> I believe we have a very clear source in the Bible itself. We are told that when the Jews were surrounded by Egyptians at the shore of the Red Sea, God assured them that they did not have to be afraid. The Lord would fight for them and destroy their enemy. And He added, "Fear not, stand still, and see the salvation of the LORD, which He will work for you to-day; for as you see the Egyptians today, you shall not see them again *for all time*" [Exodus 14:13]. The divine promise was that they would never again see the Egyptians. Yet several sentences later, after the sea miraculously split for the Jews and then drowned the Egyptians, the Bible records that the dead were washed up on shore so the children of Israel could be certain that those who pursued them had really perished. "Thus the LORD saved Israel that day out of the hand of the Egyptians; and *Israel saw the Egyptians dead upon the sea-shore*" [Exodus 14:30].
>
> Clearly this proves that seeing a corpse isn't the same as seeing the person.

The rabbis immediately agreed that this was a legitimate proof. They permitted the man who wanted to reassert his friendship to assist in this final mitzvah (religious obligation). And the law attested to the truth that must guide us as we regard the mortal remains of those whom we love: a person is not defined by a body—just as a jewelry box containing a precious diamond within it is hardly identical to its priceless content.

The body was the house of the deceased while on earth. Now it is merely a vacant former residence.

Some religions permit viewing the body as a reminder of the person we knew. Judaism forbids it. The coffin must remain closed. The reason? We shouldn't confuse the body we see before us with the reality of the vibrant human being who added so much to our lives.

Jews perform an interesting symbolic ritual in response to the death of a loved one. It is called *kriah*—making a rip in one's garment. People think the purpose is to allow physical release, to tear something as a sign of anger. That is not the way the mystics of the Kabbalah explain this ritual.

The relationship between garment and body symbolically parallels the connection between body and soul. Clothing covers us; it isn't our essence or our identity. If a garment we wear gets ripped, it doesn't actually affect us. Our true selves remain intact. So too, our bodies are the "garments" of our soul. They are external to it; one is independent of the other.

Death is the rending of our outer garment. But it is no more than that.

That's why the mourners perform the mitzvah of *kriah*, to affirm that as painful as the loss of a loved one may be, there is great comfort in knowing that "the ripping of the garment" hasn't diminished the actual person.

Yet even as I've made much of the fact that death diminishes the significance of the body, we shouldn't fail to take note of the ways in which NDE testimonies, as well as the teachings of Kabbalah, emphasize the powerful linkage that remains even after death severs the connection between the physical remains and the soul.

The soul owes its life on earth to the body. For a long time, the two of them coexist in a mutually beneficial relationship. When the soul departs at death, it does so in stages. It hesitates before bidding final farewell to its physical partner. Like a magnet, the soul continues to be drawn to the site of its former longtime residence.

As we've noted, the soul is fully aware of everything that's happening below as it gazes down from a spot above its previous home. It stays close to the body, finding it difficult to accept the reality of ultimate separation.

Almost all religions and cultures acknowledge the relationship between body and soul that extends beyond death. In Judaism there is particular sensitivity to the soul's concern for respectful treatment of "the earthly garment" that enabled it to carry out its life's mission.

The body is carefully washed, even though it will soon disintegrate. For as long as possible, it needs to be accorded the dignity it earned during life. The body retains its right to modesty; only women may prepare a female body for burial and only men a male. The corpse is to be put into a closed coffin so that onlookers are not left with the memory of a diminished human being.

More striking still, Jewish law forbids those in the immediate presence of the dead to eat and drink or to fulfill a mitzvah—because that would be mocking them, inasmuch as they are now incapable of doing the same!

The corpse may not know or care. But the soul of the departed does. Honoring the body is a way of showing our respect for the soul that remains close by until it's assured its partner received proper treatment.

Knowing this has also always made me feel the awesome responsibility for delivering a eulogy. To sum up the meaning of a life in the usually short time period allotted is difficult enough. To know the soul of the departed is among the listeners makes it almost impossible to do justice to the task.

When done well, I find myself uneasy to have people compliment me with the words, "If only he were alive to hear it." I fully believe the deceased hear every word. My hope always is that they aren't upset, either by my having said too much or too little.

The link between body and soul weakens with time. Jewish tradition maintains that the soul remains very close until burial, hovers near the family during the time of *shivah*, the seven days of mourning, and continues to maintain a connection to the grave site—allowing family members and friends to feel its presence when they visit—even as it shifts its "primary residence" to another location.

That ultimate location is the one from which no living person has ever returned. For that reason, we have no direct testimony about the next world. As we try to delve into the secrets of heaven and hell and the world to come, we will have to rely upon faith, the accrued wisdom of the ages, and the mystical traditions of the Kabbalah that claim, each in their own way, to offer us the answers.

12

HEAVEN AND HELL

And many of those who sleep in the dust of the earth shall
awake,
Some to everlasting life,
Some to shame and contempt.

—Daniel 12:2

Does it really make a big difference if we get to heaven?

Oh yes, I'm sure it makes a hell of a difference—with apologies for my feeble attempt to inject some humor into a most serious issue.

Throughout history, most people have believed in heaven and hell. Roughly seven out of ten (72 percent) Americans today say they believe in heaven—defined as a place "where people who have led good lives are eternally rewarded," according to the Pew Research Center's 2014 Religious Landscape Study. At the same time, 58 percent of U.S. adults also believe in hell—a place "where people who have led bad lives and die without being sorry are eternally punished."

There's no way to know for certain. Heaven and hell both remain in the realm of uncharted territories, their very existence controversial and disputed.

But let me share with you what I believe based on the explorations of faith, mystical teachings, wisdom of the ancients, and insights of newly revealed NDE disclosures.

I believe in heaven because souls that survive have to be somewhere—and heaven is what we call our "continued existence" after life, together with our friends, family, and loved ones who predeceased us.

Heaven is the place to which those who had near-death experiences were speeding before they were stopped in order to complete their mission on earth, the place they perceived from a distance as incredibly bright, beautiful, and joyous.

Heaven is the place where our finite years are finally understood for their meaning and purpose.

Heaven is the place where God can at last rectify the wrongs we undeservedly endured, demonstrate His commitment to justice, and fulfill the rewards He promised us that didn't materialize while we were still alive.

Heaven is what we intuitively understand is part of the divine scheme of creation without which the world and everything in it do not make sense.

Heaven is what the prophets assured us exists.

And heaven with all of its blessings is the only reality that can validate our belief in a kind, loving, and fair God.

Ask me what heaven is like, and I'll tell you I know what it isn't. Without our bodies, there can't be any physical pleasures.

The great Jewish philosopher of the Middle Ages, Maimonides, stated the Jewish view clearly:

Life in the world to come does not involve a body or an inner body. The world to come is inhabited by souls of the righteous people without their bodies, like the ministering angels. Since they do not have any bodies they don't need to eat or drink, nor do they need to do any of the things which men's bodies in this world need, and nor do they do any of the things which people in this world do with their bodies, such as standing, sitting, sleeping, dying, feeling pain, acting frivolously, et cetera. The first Sages said that in the World to Come there is no eating, drinking or coition, but that the righteous people sit with their crowns on their heads and benefit from the radiance of the Divine Presence. This shows that because there is no eating or drinking there is no [physical] body. When they said that the righteous people sit they meant it figuratively, i.e. the righteous people are there, without laboring or pains. Similarly, when they said that the righteous people have crowns on their heads they were referring to the knowledge because of which they inherited a place in the World to Come. This knowledge is always with them, as is their crown, as Solomon said, ". . . with the crown with which his mother crowned him." It is also written, ". . . and everlasting joy shall be upon their head"—this is not physical pleasure which they will receive, but the crown of the Sages, i.e. knowledge. When they said that they will benefit from the radiance of the Divine Presence they meant that they will know and understand the existence of God in a manner that they couldn't while in their gloomy and paltry bodies. (Mishneh Torah, Laws of Repentance, 8:2)

It's never made sense to me to think of heaven as a place where you can enjoy a great steak or even better, sex, when we certainly know we lack the physical ability to do either one of them.

(In fact, while many people have heard of the Islamic hadith about seventy-two virgins—which some Muslims claim is a "weak" hadith—they are unaware that for centuries, Muslim scholars have debated how literally to take the Qur'an's descriptions of Paradise [The Garden] and The Fire. The Mu'tazilites, in particular, read all such portrayals metaphorically. In the words of Ibn Sina, said by most scholars to have had a significant influence on Maimonides, we should understand these passages in the Qur'an as "in the soul's imagination.")

Without a body, some things just aren't possible. But life has taught me that real happiness has far more to do with our feelings than our physical pleasure. Our most joyous memories are inscribed in our minds and our hearts. The greatest moments of our lives have to do with love and emotions. And they have their source in the soul that survives even after death.

Maimonides, as a true philosopher, assumed that the greatest gift of heaven is the perfection of the intellect. For him, "sharing the radiance of the Divine Presence" means the joy of study and contemplation. His view of heaven is an Academy on High, with the Almighty as our eternal Professor. It's a vision perfectly attuned to scholars. Who's to say that that indeed isn't *their* heaven?

But perhaps heavenly rewards for righteous living aren't that restricted. Just as in life, there may be a wide variety of spiritually valid pleasures reserved for us, taking into account personal variables. What they share is their ability to provide us with indescribable happiness. And they must really be able to fulfill their goal because they have to last for eternity!

That's a vision of heaven that I can believe in.

But if heaven is a reward for leading the good life, there has to be room in our theology for belief in hell as well. Justice is just as much about punishing the wicked as it is about rewarding the righteous. The Bible constantly warns us that there are consequences to doing evil, and yet all too often the sinners seem to get away with it. Fairness demands a final accounting for all of our deeds.

That's why the idea of hell has become part of our universal heritage. But the way it's often described defies all reason.

"Hell burns," said Shakespeare in *Richard III*. The fiery furnace of everlasting damnation is a popular image, from the pages of Dante's *Inferno* to the fiery warnings (pun intended) of some evangelical preachers. Not to be outdone for imaginative torture, other traditions—perhaps derived from those more familiar with extremely frigid climates—depict brutally cold and unendurable subfreezing conditions. Extremes, from excruciating temperatures to the most brutal afflictions of pain the human mind has been able to conceive, have found their way into descriptions of the final fate awaiting sinners—all ostensibly from a kind, compassionate, and loving God!

Not surprisingly, many have found it impossible to reconcile the ethical ideals of the Bible with the horrors of hell. "There is one very serious defect to my mind in Christ's moral character, and that is that He believed in hell," wrote the British philosopher Bertrand Russell. The idea of eternal punishment for sin, he further notes, is "a doctrine that put cruelty in the world and gave the world generations of cruel torture."

Religious philosopher John Hick refers to hell as a "grim fantasy" that is not only "morally revolting" but also "a serious perversion of the Christian Gospel." Theologian Clark Pinnock, despite still regarding himself as an evangelical, dismisses hell with a rhetorical question: "How can one imagine for a moment that the God who gave His Son to die for sinners because of His great love for them would install a torture chamber somewhere in the new creation in order to subject those who reject Him to everlasting pain?"

What these critics of hell share is not so much a condemnation of the idea that sin warrants punishment as their unwillingness to accept the possibility of divine recompense that is both eternal and cruel beyond measure. Civilized societies condemn torture, no matter how severe the crime it is meant to punish. Can our conception of God allow for any less ethical behavior?

Hell, as conceived of in the popular imagination, is simply indefensible. Thankfully, Jewish tradition and the insights of Kabbalah offer a totally different way to understand how a God of love nonetheless conceived of a hell as an alternative to heaven.

Let's first eliminate all those horrible images of physical pain and torture. Has everyone forgotten that after death we no longer have bodies? Pain from heat or cold, from whippings or violence, from nerve endings exposed to excruciating stimuli or bone-breaking beatings—all of these are simply impossible. Just as the joys of heaven transcend physical sensations, so too the afflictions of hell have nothing to do with what we associate with pain on this earth.

How then can we be punished? Stop and think about the worst part of the times we disappointed our parents when we did something wrong. The best parents didn't resort to corporal punishment. They didn't have to lay a hand on us. They just showed how much we had hurt them and how they couldn't believe we had acted that way. They let us know they were sure we were better than our behavior indicated. They made us feel ashamed of what we did. And that shame was our greatest punishment.

God doesn't need torture to teach us to regret our wrongdoing. As He reviews our life with us—something revealed to every NDE survivor—we witness moments that make us cringe with embarrassment. How could we possibly have done that, we wonder. Our failings are revealed, and we feel as mortified as those who, in the most common of nightmares, see themselves naked in a social gathering. From the perspective of spiritual hindsight, we wish more than anything else we could undo our wrongs. We grieve for our sins and feel intense pain for our failures. That pain, that self-inflicted hurt that comes from knowing how much we upset God by not living up to our divine potential, is the hell we have to endure for having messed up our lives.

Kabbalah explains that it is not God who judges us in the end. It is we ourselves who are entrusted with that task. Our only restriction is that we must do it honestly. Which is why a verdict of guilty, as final confession, is so much more meaningful and so much more personally painful.

Hell is God's way of giving us a time-out to reflect and to repent. The goal isn't to make us suffer but to make us renounce the evils of our past in order to purify our souls.

And there's one more major misconception about hell from a Jewish and Kabbalistic perspective. Popular thinking has adopted Dante's sign before the entrance to hell that reads, "Abandon hope all ye who enter here." Damnation is eternal with no possibility for parole. Can there be anything harsher than that?

I cannot believe that. My faith tells me I don't have to. Hell is a purification *process,* with a predetermined maximum sentence. The longest stay is twelve months. That's what's required to cleanse a soul that has become sullied to the very worst possible extent. The less "cleansing" the soul needs, the shorter the mandatory time before it's deemed fit to make its way to heaven.

The book of Ecclesiastes tells us: "There is no man so righteous on earth who does only good and never sins" (7:20). Perfection is a human impossibility. All of us in some measure stain our divine souls. For that, we need the purification that defines the purpose of hell. It may be a moment, a day, or a month—but no matter what, it cannot exceed a year.

The Jewish ritual of Kaddish alludes to this truth. Mourners pray for the deceased in the hope that their demonstration of ongoing love accrues, to the merit of the soul being judged. Kaddish is recited for eleven months and no more. Why just eleven months? The maximum time it might serve any purpose is twelve months, the very longest time anyone, even the most wicked, hasn't yet made it to heaven. To say Kaddish for the entire twelve months would be casting aspersions on a person's character, implying the possibility of a maximum sentence. We refuse to allow for that suggestion. On the other hand . . . Who knows? There may be some who come close to needing our prayers for a very long time. The decision we've come to is to settle on eleven months. Long enough to assuredly include anyone we care for, without ignoring the possibility of some sins we were unaware of that require lengthier purification.

Yes, even a God of love punishes. So do wise parents and teachers. All of us can only grow and mature if we accept the fact that there are consequences to our actions, be they during our lifetimes or in the world beyond.

But these punishments are reasonable. Their purpose is not punitive but redemptive. They ought not be confused with physical pain but rather with spiritual growth. Their affliction comes from personal recognition of our failures. Their instruction makes us hurt even as our souls begin to heal.

And most important of all, the pain of hell comes with an expiration date. No one should ever abandon hope—because that's not the way heaven works.

13

WHO MAKES IT TO HEAVEN?

The righteous of all the nations of the world have a share in the world to come.

—Jerusalem Talmud, Sanhedrin

There's something about heaven that frightens me.

Is it possible I won't get in because it's a restricted community?

There are so many different religions in the world. Many of them claim not only sole possession of Truth but the right for *their* adherents alone to enter the pearly gates leading to eternal bliss.

Heaven, the theory goes, has a "keep out" sign for a goodly portion of mankind. If you had the right faith during your lifetime, you are eligible to get in. If by some accident of birth or upbringing you failed to worship God by his "right" name, you flunk the entrance requirement no matter how righteous or saintly a life you may have lived.

You might think belief in a universal God, a God who created all of us in His image, would lead to a heaven populated by all of His children. But somehow sectarianism has triumphed over a sense of the brotherhood and sisterhood of all mankind. All too many theologies persist in adhering to the principle that "it's my way or the highway"—you either agree or you're doomed to hell.

Years ago, a rabbinic colleague shared a remarkable story with me. He was a chaplain in the United States Army during World War II. On the base with him, serving as a chaplain for Catholics, was a very pleasant and charming priest. In no time at all, they became the best of friends, sharing almost everything except their religious convictions. One day, the priest told the rabbi that he had to discuss something extremely important with him.

"You know how much I love you," the priest said. "I can't imagine the day coming when I leave this world knowing that we will never meet again. You won't be able to be with me in heaven because you don't believe in Jesus. I beg of you—can't you get yourself to believe that Jesus is the Savior so that we can spend eternity together?"

How beautiful to see a strong friendship between spiritual leaders of two different faiths. How sad to realize that a theology of exclusion required one of them to believe that death would forcibly separate them.

For centuries, traditional Christian dogma taught that as non-believers in the divinity of Jesus, Jews could not be expected to get past the pearly gates. Salvation was promised only to a clearly defined and limited group: "Those who believe in him are not condemned; but those who do not believe are condemned already, because they have not believed in the name of the only son of God" (John 3:18).

More recently, Pastor Rob Bell, head of an evangelical mega-church in Michigan, has sparked much discussion as well as debate in Christian circles by preaching the gospel of universalism. In his controversial bestseller *Love Wins: A Book about Heaven, Hell, and the Fate of Every Person Who Ever Lived,* Bell challenges the notion of heaven as an exclusive country club that would be condemned on earth for its political incorrectness and intolerance.

Exclusivity in a pluralistic world is something that Pastor Bell finds hard to justify. A God of love, it seems to him, could make room in His eternal abode for those who led lives of goodness even if they were spiritually misguided in their beliefs.

(Interestingly, in *Islam and the Fate of Others: The Salvation Question*, Mohammad Hassan Khalil examines four of the most prominent figures in the history of Islam—Ghazali, Ibn 'Arabi, Ibn Taymiyya, and Rashid Rida—and makes a convincing case that, while considering Islamic faith superior, their belief in God's mercy and justice led them to believe in a Paradise populated by Muslims and non-Muslims.)

And while this may seem dangerous and perhaps even heretical to some religious followers, it is in fact a fundamental premise of Judaism. For Jews, it is what one does that is far more important than what one believes. That's why Jewish theology proclaims that "the righteous of all the nations of the world have a share in the world to come."

What seems to have escaped notice in this contemporary controversy is that the concept of a universalistic heaven open to all had a powerful spokesman long before Pastor Bell, in the very heart of the Vatican itself. As my coauthor Roy Doliner and I revealed in our book *The Sistine Secrets: Michelangelo's Forbidden Messages in the Heart of the Vatican*, discreetly tucked into a corner of one of the world's most famous paintings, in none other than the Sistine Chapel, Michelangelo had the courage to defy the teachings of the church of his time and proclaim the very same message.

Twenty-three years after Michelangelo completed his magnificent frescoes on the ceiling of the Sistine Chapel, he was called back by Pope Clement VII to redo the front wall of the chapel with a monumental version of *The Last Judgment*. For seven long years, Michelangelo labored to portray the moment when Jesus returns to earth to judge all souls, the righteous to ascend to heaven, and the evil ones to be damned to eternal punishment in hell.

At the very top of this masterpiece, we see the Angels holding the instruments of Christ's martyrdom. Just below the level of these Angels are the Righteous Souls, forming a circle over the head of Jesus. These are not the famous saints or popes or royal patrons that one would normally find in a painting of this kind. Instead, these are the true holy souls, mostly unknown in life and rewarded in the afterlife, mingling with the Angels around Christ. A fascinating detail usually overlooked—and quite possibly intentionally so—was clearly inserted by the artist to express his deeply held personal belief about salvation. Directly over Jesus's head is a handsome golden-haired Angel robed in red, pointing at two men in this inner circle of the righteous. They are obviously Jews.

One is wearing the two-pointed hat that the church forced Jewish males to wear to reinforce the medieval prejudice that Jews, being spawn of the devil, had horns. While speaking to the other, older Jew, he makes the very same gesture we find Noah making on the Sistine ceiling: pointing one finger upward, to indicate the oneness of God. The other Jew is wearing a yellow cap of shame, the kind that, in 1215, the church ordered Jewish men to wear in public. In front of them is a woman, with her hair modestly covered, who is whispering in the ear of a nude youth before her. The youth resembles Michelangelo's young tutor Giovanni Pico della Mirandola, who shared with the artist his positive views of Jews as well as his universalistic belief in a God whose love embraced all of mankind.

For Michelangelo, as for Pastor Bell, there is no divine prejudice in the afterlife. And thankfully, that is a view gaining more and more credibility.

It is fascinating to realize how much Michelangelo's insights of half a millennium ago have found their way into contemporary theological thought. When *Time* magazine, in 2009, featured the cover story "The 10 Ideas That Are Changing the World"—on the ten most powerful ideas that are changing the way we think and that have the most potential for impacting our future—it singled out the movement in current religious scholarship toward "re-Judaizing Jesus." Calling it a "seismic change" in today's seminaries across the Christian spectrum, it identified the new trend toward acknowledging Jesus's Judaism and recognizing the Jewish roots of Christians' faith, the very ideas that Michelangelo so desperately sought to incorporate into his masterpiece on the Sistine Chapel ceiling. Contemporary theologians are devoting their efforts to finding common ground between faiths so that all of God's children may live together in brotherhood on earth—as they hopefully do in heaven.

The really good news is that perhaps one of the most significant revelations from near-death experiences is confirmation for those who take the side of a universalistic heaven.

Those who "passed on" and were shown a glimpse of the afterlife, as we've noted, were greeted by friends and family who predeceased them. These heavenly residents reassured them, told them not to be worried and to await unparalleled bliss.

Now here's the point that needs to be stressed: *The near-death experience has been reported by people of all faiths, and their greeters from heaven span the gamut of countless different religions.*

If we take these reports seriously—as so many religious people today do because of their affirmation of an afterlife—we must equally acknowledge the message they send of a heaven free from prejudice and spiritual exclusion.

True, those who are Christian report meeting Jesus. On the other hand, Jews who recount their experiences speak of meeting Moses. All of them see God represented by the deity they had been worshiping during their lifetime. Yet all of them experience a divine encounter.

In recent decades, some prominent theologians such as the late German Jesuit priest Karl Rahner have wrestled with the question whether non-Christians can be saved through their own religions. Rosemary Keller, professor of church history at the Union Theological Seminary in Manhattan, concludes that "theological pluralism is very much the effect of our global village." And in a much-publicized movement in the Reformed Church in America, Reverend Richard Rhem invokes the image of a cathedral with stained-glass windows. Inside stand groups of Jews, Christians, and Muslims. Each group reads the story of its faith in a particular window. All the windows, he said, are illuminated by the light of God.

The Vatican as well, at the Second Vatican Council in 1965, made historic changes to church policies and theology. Among them was *Nostra Aetate*, Latin for "In Our Time," a document that revolutionized the Catholic Church's approach to Jews and Judaism after nearly two thousand years. Section four of *Nostra Aetate* repudiates the centuries-old "deicide" charge against all Jews, stresses the religious bond shared by Jews and Catholics, reaffirms the eternal covenant between God and the People of Israel, and dismisses church interest in trying to baptize Jews. The late Pope John Paul II described the declaration *Nostra Aetate* that emanated from the Second Vatican Ecumenical Council as "an expression of Faith" and "an inspiration of the Holy Spirit, as a word of Divine Wisdom." In keeping with Pope John Paul II's statements, Cardinal Walter Kasper, president of the Holy See's Commission for Religious Relations with Jewry, stated in an address at Boston College in November 2002: "This does not mean that Jews in order to be saved have to become Christians; if they follow their own conscience and believe in God's promises as they understand them in their religious tradition, they are in line with God's plan, which for us came to its historical completion in Jesus Christ."

I can personally testify to the new spirit of mutual spiritual recognition. In January of 2005, I had the honor of leading a delegation of 150 rabbis to meet with Pope John Paul II, at his invitation, in the Apostolic Palace. We were told that this was perhaps the most historic meeting between Christians and Jews in all of history. Three rabbis, I among them, blessed the Pope. He in turn acknowledged us as "his older brothers in faith" and stressed our ties of brotherhood under one universal God.

Rabbi Benjamin Blech with Pope John Paul II
Photo courtesy of the author

Different stained-glass windows illuminated by the light of the same creator.

That was a moment of heaven on earth. And that, I am certain, is what the real heaven looks like as well.

14

ENCORE?

All pure and holy spirits live on in heavenly places, and in course of time they are again sent down to inhabit righteous bodies.

—Josephus, Jewish historian

We can only wonder if our souls not only survive after death but also have an opportunity to return to earth.

The idea of reincarnation goes back many millennia. The Greek philosophers Plato and Pythagoras, among many others, as well as the druids and Egyptians before them, all believed in reincarnation.

Vilified as rank superstition in some quarters, reincarnation is a major belief of Hinduism, which has grown to become the world's third-largest religion, after Christianity and Islam. It claims about 950 million followers—about 14 percent of the world's population—and is the dominant religion in India, Nepal, and among the Tamils in Sri Lanka.

According to a 2005 Gallup poll, 20 percent of U.S. adults believe in reincarnation. Recent surveys by the Barna Group, a Christian research nonprofit organization, have found that a quarter of U.S. Christians, including 10 percent of all born-again Christians, embrace the idea. Feature films such as *Kundun*, *What Dreams May Come*, and *Birth*; contemporary books by authors such as Carol Bowman, Brian Weiss, and Vicki Mackenzie; as well as popular songs, regularly mention reincarnation.

Once again, the evidence for something impossible to prove scientifically is primarily anecdotal. Yet who is to say that anecdotal evidence confirming truths long taught by mystical traditions including the Kabbalah doesn't deserve serious consideration?

The pioneer of contemporary reincarnation research is Dr. Ian Stevenson. The former head of the Department of Psychiatry at the University of Virginia, he is now director of the Division of Perceptual Studies at the University of Virginia. Stevenson has devoted the last forty years to the scientific documentation of past-life memories of children from all over the world and has over three thousand cases in his files. Many people, including skeptics and scholars, agree that these cases offer the best evidence yet for reincarnation.

Dr. Stevenson's research into the possibility of reincarnation began in 1960, when he heard of a case in Sri Lanka where a child claimed to remember a past life. He thoroughly questioned the child and the child's parents, as well as the people whom the child claimed were his parents in a past life. This led to his conviction that reincarnation might very well be a reality.

The more cases he pursued, the greater became his drive to document these cases.

He believed he could furnish proof of its reality in a way that could satisfy scientific criteria.

In 1960, Dr. Stevenson published two articles in the *Journal of the American Society for Psychical Research* about children who remembered past lives. In 1974, he published *Twenty Cases Suggestive of Reincarnation*, and in 1997, Dr. Stevenson followed this with *Reincarnation and Biology*, covering thirty years of his ongoing research. One of the most fascinating aspects he uncovered involving children's memories of past lives was that *these children frequently bore lasting birthmarks that supposedly related to their murder or the death they suffered in a previous life.* Stevenson's research into birthmarks and congenital defects has particular importance for the demonstration of reincarnation since it furnishes objective and graphic proof of reincarnation, superior to the—often fragmentary—memories and reports of the children and adults questioned, which even if verified afterward, cannot be assigned the same value in scientific terms.

Dr. Brian Weiss, chairman emeritus of the Department of Psychiatry at the Mount Sinai Medical Center in Miami and clinical associate professor of psychiatry at the University of Miami School of Medicine, is another prominent physician who came to believe in reincarnation quite by accident. In 1980, one of his patients, "Catherine," began discussing past-life experiences under hypnosis. At the time, Weiss didn't believe in reincarnation, but after confirming elements of Catherine's past-life stories through research into public records, he became convinced of the survival of an element of the human personality after death. Since 1980, Weiss claims he has regressed more than four thousand patients. Today he advocates the therapeutic benefits of hypnotic regression, noting his belief that many present-life phobias and ailments are rooted in past-life experiences that—when acknowledged by the patient—have a curative effect on the present-life condition.

Weiss's books on the subject, *Many Lives, Many Masters: The True Story of a Prominent Psychiatrist, His Young Patient, and the Past-Life Therapy That Changed Both Their Lives* (1988); *Same Soul, Many Bodies: Discover the Healing Power of Future Lives through Progression Therapy* (2005); and *Regression through the*

Mirrors of Time (Meditation Regression) (2008) have combined sales of many millions of copies around the world.

The belief in reincarnation seems to be the best way to account for the genius of infant and child prodigies. As Frank Curtiss points out, "Infant prodigies manifest their amazing talents even before their brains are fully developed." The ability of Mozart to play the piano at two years of age and write a sonata at four and an opera at eight can't be explained by heredity. Joseph Hoffman gave such marvelous improvisations, of themes suggested without notice, that he was considered a master of the piano at age ten. In fact, many consider him a reincarnation of Mozart. The mentally deficient young boy known as Blind Tom never had a music lesson but could accurately reproduce the most difficult piece of music after hearing it played but once. The uneducated shepherd boy Zerah Colburn, at the age of eight, could perform such marvelous mathematical feats as mentally extracting the cube root of numbers in the hundreds of millions and the square root of numbers containing six figures. He instantly gave the correct number of minutes in forty-eight years. Pascal, at the age of two, demonstrated mathematical problems with diagrams. At the age of six, he wrote the most learned treatise on conic sections that had yet appeared. William Hamilton began the study of Hebrew at three, and at thirteen, he knew thirteen languages. The list goes on and on. Exceedingly great intellect, even in the rarefied atmosphere of IQs above 180, could still not account for these incredible accomplishments. These prodigies must be the result of causes that cannot be explained either by heredity or environment. The only explanation that remains is that these were capabilities brought over from previous lives.

Kabbalah insists that is true. Many have mistakenly claimed that the concept of reincarnation has no source in Judaism. That is not correct. It has long been a part of the oral tradition. The

Zohar, the classic work of Jewish mysticism, makes frequent and lengthy reference to it. Rabbinical scholars throughout the ages incorporated the concept into their commentaries. Nachmanides (Ramban, 1195–1270), attributed Job's suffering to reincarnation, as hinted in Job's saying, "'God does all these things twice or three times with a man, to bring back his soul from the pit to . . . the light of the living'" (Job 33:29, 30). Although the Bible chose not to reveal the truth of reincarnation to us directly, many people have nonetheless felt it intuitively.

While in some religions its affirmation is mandatory, neither Judaism nor Christianity makes it a prerequisite of faith. Yet it offers a powerful response to the problem of theodicy, the lack of reward for the righteous or punishment for the wicked during our lifetimes.

What we see may not be the full story. What is left unresolved in Act I of one life may very well be rectified in acts that follow.

Kabbalah sees reincarnation as serving many additional purposes: it permits us a second opportunity to face up to challenges that may have previously defeated us. It's somewhat like the story of the opera singer whose rather mediocre performance was greeted with loud shouts of "encore" from the audience. After repeating the aria, again to the same response, he thanked the people but graciously declined, only to have the crowd yell out, "Encore, encore—you'll do it till you get it right."

An example the rabbis of the Kabbalah offer to illustrate reincarnation in order to rectify a weakness of a previous lifetime is that of biblical Jacob. Jacob led an exemplary life, but he failed in one shameful way.

In Genesis 33:1–3 we read:

> And Jacob lifted up his eyes and looked, and behold, Esau came and with him four hundred men. And he divided the

children among Leah and Rachel and the two handmaids. And
he put the handmaids and their children foremost, and Leah
and her children after, and Rachel and Joseph hindmost. And
he passed over before them, and bowed himself to the ground
seven times until he came near to his brother.

A righteous man who puts his trust in God ought never to bow
down to a fellow human being. Jacob's bowing is considered sin-
ful.

Many generations later, in the book of Esther, we read the
story of Mordecai. One characteristic is singled out as a sign of his
greatness. In Chapter 3:1–4 we read:

After these things did King Ahasuerus promote Haman the son
of Hammedatha the Agagite, and advanced him and set his seat
above all the princes who were with him. And all the king's
servants who were in the king's gate bowed and reverenced
Haman, for the king had so commanded concerning him. But
Mordecai bowed not, nor did him reverence. Then the king's
servants, who were in the king's gate, said unto Mordecai,
"Why transgressest thou the king's commandment?" Now it
came to pass, when they spoke daily unto him and he heark-
ened not unto them, that they told Haman to see whether
Mordecai's matters would stand; for he had told them that he
was a Jew.

Here is a biblical sequel to the Jacob story that illustrates the truth
that Jews are meant to bow only to God. Out of fear, Jacob had
bowed several times to his wicked brother, Esau. He was wrong.
Mordecai's mission in life was to demonstrate this central teaching. His soul was a reincarnation of the biblical ancestor who required another lifetime in order to atone for his one major failing.

Perhaps most powerfully, the concept of reincarnation has
been used by a rabbinic scholar in Israel today to explain a con-

temporary phenomenon unique in Jewish history. There has never been a time when so many Jews from secular backgrounds have turned to religion. What explains this dramatic shift to spirituality? The answer he offers is that we are in the age of post-Holocaust Jewry. We follow a time when six million Jews perished, one-third of them infants and children who died before their appointed time. They should have had an opportunity to live out their lives within their religious tradition. Deprived because of the evil of others, God decided to provide them with another chance. They were reborn to live out their lives anew. There weren't enough religious homes to which their souls could be sent, so they were born to secular parents. But their souls knew their origins and were determined to re-create their former spiritual lives. *The returnees to faith of this generation are the reincarnated souls of the six million.*

A daring interpretation indeed!

We need not accept it at face value. We need only to acknowledge that it is possible.

Belief in reincarnation is a way of emphasizing our faith in a God who is committed to the same ideal we prize from our fellow human beings: "Give me another chance," we plead on many occasions. It's very comforting to discover that in certain instances, God agrees.

15

THE FIVE MAJOR LESSONS

Everything has an appointed season, and there is a
Time for every matter under the heaven . . .
A time to give birth and a time to die; a time to
Plant and a time to uproot that which is planted.

—Ecclesiastes 2:1–2

Life is a thorough university; pain and hardship are its distinguished professors.

—Matshona Dhliwayo

I've learned much in my life. Some of my knowledge came from school. Other parts came from books, from professors and teachers, from parents and friends. Most, however, of what I would call wisdom came from experience—from coping with life and its challenges, its difficulties and its hardships, its trials and its pains.

Among the events that, in retrospect, blessed me with the greatest understanding is the one that prompted the writing of this book. The diagnosis of my imminent death is what led me to the most profound insights about life.

Until now I have shared with you many truths about death and dying.

Let me now share the five major lessons about living I have learned since my doctor stamped me with an expiration date.

The one thing you need to know, however, before you continue reading, is the amazing reality that made these words possible: I did not die as predicted. I was given six months—and it is now six years later. My doctors are perplexed. The diagnosis of my condition was not an error. My cardiac amyloidosis is still there, having stopped progressing any further as if divinely forbidden from carrying out its nefarious objective. Remarkably—and inexplicably—I feel fine, continuing to carry on with a full-time teaching schedule as well as writing and lecturing in communities around the world.

My doctors wonder, how is that possible? I have become "the poster boy" for medical miracles. I know that I will not live forever—even as I no longer fear dying—but I also recognize that something special has happened that defies easy explanation. I am not the same person I was six years ago. Today I fully grasp the words of Paulo Coelho: "Life always waits for some crisis to occur before revealing itself at its most brilliant." I have learned the truth of the maxim that "being challenged in life is inevitable; being defeated is optional." And so, before this book comes to a close, let me tell you the secrets of my survival—the keys to opening the door to a life filled with hope rather than fear, with happiness rather than sorrow.

REALIZING THE POWER OF FAITH

The first thing I did was grieve.

A day later, a talk with a colleague totally changed my attitude. He shared with me an amazing statistic he heard from one of his congregants, a world-renowned surgeon and cancer specialist.

Among all of his patients, every one of whom was diagnosed as incurable, the only ones who surprisingly survived were those who shared one characteristic: they had faith. It was the medical specialist, not the rabbi, who put it into these words: "Perhaps the most important thing I have learned in all the years of my practice is something I can't explain by way of my medical training but I know to be true beyond question: Faith is the most powerful medicine we possess for survival."

Let me be clear. Of course faith does not ensure overcoming death; people with faith still die. The point is simply that those who lack faith—not necessarily spiritual faith in God or a higher power but faith in their ability to overcome their present crisis— are almost certainly doomed.

To defeat an illness, just as with any other opponent, one must believe in the possibility of victory. Accepting death as inevitable is a great part of what can actually make it come true.

In fact, Jewish law forbids doctors from ever making a statement that includes a pronouncement about the amount of time a patient has left to live. The Bible gives doctors permission to heal. It does not allow them to assume the mantle of prophet and predict when people will pass away.

I will never forget—nor forgive myself—for my greatest error of judgment in the early years of my service as congregational rabbi. It was immediately after the horrible effects of thalidomide made themselves known, a drug that never should have been approved and was routinely prescribed in the 1950s to help pregnant women cope with morning sickness but ended up causing babies to be born with deformities, who are still referred to as "thalidomide babies." Without warning, doctors around the country began to see malformed infants, babies with deformed eyes, limbs, urinary and alimentary tracts, and other serious complications. One of them was born in Oceanside, Long Island, to a member of my congregation.

You can well imagine the pain of the parents. Shortly after the birth, the doctor in charge took me aside and with the authoritative air of his profession told me what I, as their rabbi, had the obligation to advise them on. This "thing," which he refused even to dignify with the word *baby*, had no chance to survive for more than a short time. "It" will never be able to physically or mentally develop in any meaningful way. It would be best for the mother not to form any attachment to "it" in order to ease the agony of a relationship doomed only to suffering and early separation. And so he asked me to get their permission to "remove it" with instructions for "minimal care"—a euphemism for murder.

I find it hard to write the following words. In my defense, I was a very young rabbi cowed by a medical professional many years my senior. But, sad to say, I did what he asked. I phrased it not as a rabbinic decision but nonetheless as my suggestion. Thankfully, God intervened. The parents were people of great faith who in this instance had far better judgment than I did. They told me what I should have said. The doctor's job is to heal. If he cannot do that, he should step aside and let God take charge of what follows. We, the parents told me, have faith, and we will do whatever is in our power to preserve our child's life and make it as meaningful as possible. If and when God wants her, let Him be the one to take her.

And that is exactly what they did. The "it" grew up to be a beautiful young girl who walked and talked and did everything the doctors assured us she would never be able to do. Yes, she had disabilities, but they only made her stronger. She lacked full use of some of her limbs, but she developed enough of her mind to become a lawyer—practicing and successful to this day.

Faith achieved the impossible.

I should have remembered that story when I was temporarily overwhelmed by my own personal crisis. My colleague sharing the words of the cancer specialist—"Faith is the most powerful medicine we possess for survival"—reminded me. It was then that I took a personal vow. I would not help the Angel of Death perform his task sooner than absolutely required by divine decree, not by medical prophecy. At the very least, my faith would dispel my fear.

And that was my first step, if not in recovery at least in tranquil and serene survival.

REALIZING THE POWER OF PURPOSE

A phrase that has made its way into popular culture is the "bucket list." What is a bucket list? It is a list of all the goals you want to achieve, dreams you want to fulfill, and life experiences you desire to experience before you die.

Google it and you will find lists with countless suggestions. They are invariably filled with ideas about travel to places you've never been, adventures you've never had, people you've never met. The common denominator is a beautiful idea: "The only people who fear death are those with regrets."

What's wrong with the way most people think of a bucket list is that far too often, its chief concern is the self. It's trying to figure out what we've missed out on in terms of personal enjoyment.

What I found myself thinking of, when I believed I would shortly die, was what I could do to make myself worthy in God's eyes of longer life. Not because I am a rabbi but because I sincerely believe that everyone has to recognize that they are put here on earth for a purpose. It's imperative to identify the reason for our presence in the world—what it is that we contribute to society at large and composes our legacy for the future. Then we have to

pursue that purpose in a way that would make our absence noticeable and, for as long as possible, our disappearance impossible.

I can best explain it by way of a remarkable story.

A century ago the world revered a great symphony conductor,
an Italian maestro named Arturo Toscanini (1867–1957), who led
concerts all over the world. He was known as an absolute perfec-
tionist and had few peers. Toscanini had a biographer who would
interview him periodically over the years as a part of a major book
he was writing. One evening, he called Toscanini and told him that
he would be in town the next night, and asked if he could come to
the house to interview him. Toscanini answered that he could not
because he would be doing something special that would require
absolute concentration; he could not be interrupted.

"Maestro," the biographer said, "what are you doing that's so
special?"

"There is a concert being played overseas. I used to be the
conductor of that symphony orchestra, but I could not be there
this year. So I'm going to listen on a shortwave radio and hear how
the other conductor leads the orchestra. I don't want any interrup-
tions whatsoever."

"Maestro, it would be my greatest pleasure to watch how you
listen to a concert played by an orchestra that you used to lead. I
promise I won't say anything. I'll sit on the other side of the room,
quietly."

"You promise to be perfectly quiet?" Toscanini asked.

"Yes."

"Then you can come." The next night, the biographer came and
sat quietly while Toscanini listened to the concert, which lasted
almost an hour. Finally, when it ended, the biographer remarked,
"Wow, wasn't that magnificent?"

Toscanini said, "Not really."

"Why not?"

"They were supposed to be 120 musicians, including 15 violinists. Only 14 of them played."

The biographer thought he was joking. How could he know from six thousand miles away, over shortwave radio, that one of the violinists was missing? The biographer had his doubts but didn't want to say anything and went home.

The next morning, though, he had to find out for himself, so he called the concert hall overseas, asked for the music director, and inquired as to how many musicians were supposed to have been playing the night before versus how many had actually shown up. The concert hall director told him that there were supposed to be 120 musicians, including 15 violinists, but only 14 had shown up!

The biographer was amazed. He returned to Toscanini and said, "Sir, I owe you an apology. I thought you were just making it up the other night. But please, tell me, how could you know that one violinist was missing?"

"There is a great difference between you and me," Toscanini answered. "You're a part of the audience and to the audience everything sounds wonderful. But I'm the conductor, and the conductor has to know every note of music that has to be played. When I realized that certain notes were not being played, I knew without a doubt that one of the violinists was missing."

The story had a profound impact on me. I took its implication to heart. I have been given the gift of playing a part, small as it might be, in the symphony of life. It may seem insignificant to some. But the Conductor is intensely aware of my playing, of every note I hit correctly as well as every mistake that mars the beauty of the entire performance.

For as long as I am still a member of the orchestra, I must faithfully carry out my assigned task to the best of my ability.

So the second thing I did after my diagnosis was to try to make myself indispensable. Indispensable to the "orchestra" of the

world around me and indispensable to the "conductor" and creator of the universe. At the very least, I tried to become a better
husband, a better father and grandfather, a better teacher, rabbi,
and friend. It was the bucket list of self-improvement that might
convince God I was not yet superfluous.

And so far it worked. Somehow I'm still here, and perhaps my
realizing the power of my purpose on earth is part of the reason.

REALIZING THE POWER OF OPTIMISM

On my desk is a poster with a pointed piece of advice from the
great French philosopher and essayist Michel de Montaigne: "My
life has been full of terrible misfortunes, most of which never
happened."

I bought it right after I stopped grieving over my own death—a
death very much like the mistaken obituary printed for Mark
Twain during his lifetime to which he famously replied, "The reports of my death are greatly exaggerated."

My "diagnosis of death," even if not immediately fulfilled,
could have been followed by a life of depression and despair. It
was more than faith that saved me. It was a conscious decision to
remain optimistic, not to live as if the worst had already happened,
not to become the true definition of a pessimist—a person who is
never happy unless he is miserable.

William James, the American psychologist and philosopher, as-
tutely recognized that "pessimism is essentially a religious disease." Pessimism disagrees with the opening words of the Bible in
Genesis, which offer God's judgments on the acts of his creation.
Every day, when the Almighty created anew, He figuratively
stepped back to evaluate what He brought into being and gave His
verdict that "it was good." Then, when He finally completed His

work with the creation of Adam and Eve, the Bible tells us, "And God saw everything he had made and, behold, it was very good" (Genesis 1:31).

The pessimist disagrees. The pessimist sees only the bad. Looking at a bagel, he sees only the hole and not the bread. He is a person who thinks that the chief purpose of sunshine is to cast shadows. In short, he is what is famously called a "misfortune teller."

Optimism, on the other hand, is nothing short of a divine commandment. It is the theme of one of King David's most beautiful Psalms:

> Yea, though I walk through the valley of the shadow of death, I will fear no evil: for thou art with me; thy rod and thy staff they comfort me. Thou preparest a table before me in the presence of mine enemies: thou anointest my head with oil; my cup runneth over. Surely goodness and mercy shall follow me all the days of my life: And I will dwell in the house of the LORD forever. (Psalm 23)

Remarkably enough, it is precisely in the context of walking through the valley of the shadow of death that King David finds it possible to speak of goodness and mercy. It is when we are most in need of divine assistance that we come closest to acknowledging the heavenly presence. We dwell in the house of the Lord—how can we not be optimistic?

People may disagree about almost anything, without serious consequences. I like the Mets, you like the Yankees. I thought the movie was wonderful, and you feel it was a disappointing waste of time. Disagreements make life interesting. How boring it would be if we all reacted in exactly the same way to everything.

That's not true, however, for the controversy between optimists and pessimists. Researchers at the Mayo Clinic in Rochester, Minnesota, have confirmed what many people already believed and what I previously noted by way of my colleague's surgeon friend. In a study completed in early 2000, they concluded that optimists tend to live longer and healthier lives. After an extensive and lengthy study with a group of 839 patients who had taken a personality test in the 1960s, they graded the subjects, who had ranged in age from eighteen to eighty-four, as optimists or pessimists.

Researchers classified 124 as optimistic, 518 as mixed, and 197 as pessimistic. The study found that the optimists had a better-than-expected survival rate, and the pessimists had a 19 percent increase in the risk of death.

The researchers couldn't explain how pessimism is associated with a risk of early death, and suggested a mind–body link, with a "happiness" factor being one of the most important causes of good health.

In yet another study, published by the American Psychological Association, doctors concluded that optimism even played a crucial role in the dreaded illness of cancer. They carefully followed 238 patients with metastasized or recurrent cancer who were receiving radiation treatment for their symptoms. The most prevalent forms of cancer among them were lung and breast cancer; the least common were colorectal and gastrointestinal cancers. Assessments of the patients' optimism, pessimism, and level of depression were taken when they entered the study and twice again, four months and eight months later. In the interim, seventy patients had died by the eight-month follow-up.

The researchers concluded that there is a definite connection between pessimism and mortality. They were unanimous in their conclusion: "Our findings indicate that the endorsement of a pessimistic life orientation may function as an important risk factor for mortality among cancer patients."

Again, the researchers could not explain the precise mechanism by which pessimism affects mortality in cancer patients. They did offer the suggestion, though, that "it is possible that pessimism directly affects the endocrine and immune systems, or both."

Permit me to offer a simpler explanation: If it's true that we are created "in the image of God," then we function most successfully when we share His opinion of the world.

And that was the third way in which I fought the battle for my survival.

I subscribed to the wisdom of the Bible about optimism—advice to which William James gave contemporary meaning when he wrote, "The greatest discovery of my generation is that human beings can alter their lives by altering their attitudes of mind."

I chose to alter my life by being a "cockeyed optimist"—an optimist about the here and now as well as an optimist about the world waiting for me in the future.

REALIZING THE POWER OF MIRACLES

It was Albert Einstein who said it: "There are two ways to live. You can live as if nothing is a miracle; you can live as if everything is a miracle." Implicit in what we can call Einstein's Theory of Moral Relativity is a profoundly Jewish idea: All of life is a miracle—and it cannot be said that we are truly alive if we do not grasp the miracle of our being.

Three times daily, the prayer book of the Jew includes gratitude "for Your miracles that are with us every day." Miracles are not restricted merely to the biblical stories of Moses splitting the sea or Joshua making the sun stand still in the skies. "Miracles," as C. S. Lewis so beautifully put it, "are a re-telling in small letters of the very same story which is written across the whole world in letters too large for some of us to see."

"Seeing, hearing and feeling are miracles, and each part and tag of me is a miracle" is the way Walt Whitman expressed the same idea. Miracles, in short, are the incredible illustrations of God's power and kindness expressed on such a regular basis that we take them for granted and are no longer overwhelmed by their awesomeness.

To ask whether there are still miracles today is to question our very existence and to doubt the reality of all of the world around us.

There was a moment in my life when I felt this idea with greater intensity than any other. My wife was going into labor with our fourth child. I sat in the waiting room, as I did three times before when my daughters were being born. Those were the days when husbands took no part in the birthing process. Fathers-to-be weren't allowed to enter the room where their child was coming into the world. And so I just waited anxiously for the doctor to come and tell me the news—the gender of my child, the condition of my wife, and the customary good wishes and congratulations.

But this time it was different. For whatever reason, the doctor came out while my wife was still in the midst of contractions and asked me an unusual question: "Rabbi, have you ever been witness to death; were you ever in a room when somebody died?" I didn't understand why he asked, but I responded affirmatively. Of course, as a rabbi, I am not a stranger to death and dying. "Well then," the doctor said as he grabbed me by the hand, "I think it is time for you to be witness to the moment of life."

I did not know how I would react to the sight. I was never very good with blood. It was one of the reasons I knew I could never be a doctor. I was afraid I might faint. It turned out I need not have worried. I watched—and I witnessed a moment that forevermore stayed with me as a clear and irrefutable miracle. There before my eyes was a child, a living, breathing—and yes, crying—product of our love. And, as also became apparent, a boy after three girls, a joyous fulfillment of the obligation to "be fruitful and multiply" with both sexes.

With tears of joy, I recited the appropriate blessing thanking God for having allowed me to live to see this moment. More, I always said that I believed birth was a miracle; now, at last, I didn't just believe—I knew. Beyond a shadow of a doubt, I saw the hand of God in what people so foolishly describe merely as a natural event. Blaise Pascal's words came to mind: "It is impossible on reasonable grounds to disbelieve miracles."

I did not forget that this moment happened solely because the doctor had wanted me to view the antidote to death, to for once witness birth even as I had unfortunately been present at the time of dying. What struck me forcefully ever since was the realization that the same God is the one responsible for both of these book-ends of life. Surely, then, both must share the divine qualities of wisdom, of kindness and mercy, and of justice. We are born when we are meant to be born. Our souls are called back to our creator with similar wisdom. Birth and death must both be miracles, but miracles of different meaning.

That truth is also something that gave me great strength and comfort. I was born as a miracle. If God chooses, He will perform another miracle to prolong my life. If He decides otherwise, He will introduce me to the other miracle that awaits me.

In either case, I share the words of the rabbi who said, "I am realistic—I expect miracles." And that realism continues to sustain me with hope and confidence in the future.

REALIZING THE POWER OF PRAYER

I have saved the fifth major lesson for last. Perhaps it should have been the first. It is the most universal of responses to crises, the most intuitive reaction to difficulties beyond our control, to problems that seem beyond our capability to resolve.

My heart told me to pray. I joined a lengthy list of the most prominent of my ancestors who did precisely that when the world seemed to turn against them and their difficulties seemed insurmountable. Abraham, Isaac, and Jacob prayed. Moses prayed. The prophets prayed. King David prayed—and composed Psalms that continue to stir us and bring us closer to God to this very day. Throughout all of history, from every corner of the globe, kings and commoners, the meek and the mighty, the sinners and the saintly, turned to God for the kind of help only He is capable of granting.

Were all of them deluded? Did all of them engage in mere wishful thinking? Were their efforts to convince the Almighty to come to their aid wasted words devoid of all purpose, full of sound and fury and signifying nothing?

There is a reason why people have such a problem with prayer. It's simply because they misunderstand its basic premise.

Prayer doesn't come to change God. It comes to change us—so that God will look at us differently.

Prayer doesn't come to get something—but in order to be with Someone.

Prayer is the most important conversation of our day—because we take our problems to God before we take them to anyone else.

We talk to God in order to remind ourselves that we were created in His image—and therefore we have someone to look up to as our role model.

We talk to God because God is inside every one of us—we call it our soul—and we need to communicate with our inner selves so that we can be inspired to become all that we can be.

We talk to God as a "time-out" from our obsession with possessions and our fixation with the foolish, to remind ourselves that we become worthy of God's blessings only when we concentrate on His concerns for the holy and the sacred.

We talk to God because we are God's children—and He loves to hear from us.

We talk to God because it reminds us to depend upon Him—that miracles happen but they are the divine response to those who believe in Him.

We talk to God because it gives us the chance to express ourselves completely to Him—to regularly have the most important talk of our lives with the one who can do the most to make our lives better and more meaningful.

To ask if our prayers worked is as foolish as asking if a talk with our best friend got us everything we wanted.

Prayer is rooted in love. It strengthens our relationship with God. It alters the way we look at the world. It redefines our values. It shapes our character. It improves our personality. That's why prayer is always answered—sometimes with the words we want to hear, other times with the response we need to hear.

The medical prognosis was that I was soon to die. My prayers were a powerful source of personal comfort. They were also life changing. And it seems that God decreed that the new me deserved some more time here on earth.

The Torah, you will remember, is called the Pentateuch because it consists of five books. I find it fascinating, in the aftermath of my confrontation with death, that five lessons of life turned my crisis into a profound education. Perhaps what I have learned was worth its cost.

16

A FINAL SUMMATION

Fear not the sentence of death, remember them that have been before thee, and that come after; for this is the sentence of the Lord over all flesh.

—Ben Sira

I was sitting in the airport in Dallas, waiting for a change of flight, reading my daily page of the Talmud, when an elderly priest, readily identifiable by his collar, stopped by my seat and apologetically asked me a question. "I hope you don't mind my interrupting you. I see you are reading a Hebrew book and you are wearing a hat. Are you by any chance a rabbi?"

"Yes, I am," I responded. "Is there a special reason for your asking?" "I hope you don't think I'm out of place," he continued, "but all my life I've been hoping that someday I might meet a rabbi. This is a very special moment for me. You see, although I'm a priest I've always felt that Jews are the people of The Book and enjoy an especially close relationship with God. You are God's chosen people and as a rabbi you are one of their spiritual leaders. I've always wanted to ask a rabbi for a blessing. Would it be possible now for me to ask that you honor me with that favor?"

I cannot convey in words how moved I was by that request. Of course I gave him the blessing he asked for. I chose the priestly benediction from the Pentateuch and recited it to him in the original Hebrew. He was brought to tears.

In all humility, I understood that for him, I was the link to the original Torah. Whatever theological beliefs might separate us— and there are surely many—he recognized the unique role of Judaism, in the words of Isaiah, to serve as "a light unto the nations." Jews were the ones who stood at the foot of Mount Sinai and received the two tablets of stone with the Decalogue inscribed upon them. Jews were the direct descendants of Abraham, Isaac, and Jacob. Jews were the first to transmit the words of God from one generation to the next, ever since He initially deigned to communicate with mankind. Jews were "chosen" not to claim superiority but to accept the responsibility to convey the messages of God to the rest of mankind.

For me it was an unforgettable lesson that, in spite of centuries of anti-Semitism, there is still a profound sense of respect and admiration for the Jewish people and their teachings. It is a lesson I have had the great privilege of witnessing anew many times since. All too often, we stress the unfortunate vestiges of religious prejudice and hatred. We ought to acknowledge far more frequently the bridges of tolerance and understanding that mark contemporary dialogue between faiths.

It is a sign of the special regard others have for Jews as "The People of the Book" that I've found myself constantly being asked, "What does Judaism have to say about this?" Of the three major faiths, Judaism, Christianity, and Islam, ours is the oldest. Our oral traditions go back the furthest. In the realm of the mystical, Jewish Kabbalah lays claim to the most ancient sources.

No wonder, then, when it comes to the mystery of death, Jewish ideas and teachings are so much sought after. In this book, I tried to digest and to summarize these insights so that they could help others as much as they have helped me during this time of my confrontation with the reality of death. Just as God granted me the great honor of blessing the priest in Dallas and the Pope in Rome, I similarly feel I've been given the gift of being able to share the blessing of knowledge with you, my dear reader.

I've told you the many reasons why I am not afraid of death. Faith has replaced fear. It is a faith anchored in ancient traditions validated by striking contemporary testimony that is gaining ever-greater credibility.

But when all has been said, there is one biblical thought that remains most meaningful to me. It is the introduction to the law in Deuteronomy that prohibits excessive grief in the aftermath of death: "You are the children of the LORD your God: you shall not cut yourselves, nor make any baldness between your eyes for the dead" (14:1).

Pagan practice called for mourners to cut their flesh and to rip the hair from their heads as signs of their unbearable sorrow. The Bible forbids this. Grief must be tempered. The reason? Because "you are the children of the Lord your God." Don't imagine that death is agonizingly cruel when you know it is decreed by none other than your father! You are children of the Lord. He loves you with unbounded love. Do you then think it conceivable that He has chosen to bring His blessing of life to close with a curse? Death is our universal end and our eternal beginning. Death isn't the enemy of life—death is no more the enemy of life than sleep is the enemy of work and play. Sleep makes it possible for us to work and play the next day; it makes it possible for us to live on. In the same way, death is the gateway through which we slip from the lower life of our present existence into the higher celestial realm, from the ephemeral to the everlasting.

Jewish law requires that in response to death, we recite a verse from the book of Job: "The Lord hath given and the Lord hath taken, blessed be the name of the Lord." We don't simply state a fact, we express a profound truth. The very death that deprives us of a precious life is the result of a previous gift. The Lord proved his love for us with His original gift of life. That same Lord who gave is the one who now has taken. What He did at first out of love by giving is, if we could only understand it, just as much now His motivation for taking.

There is a magnificent story, found in the Midrash, recording a story about the Talmudic sage Rabbi Meir. One Sabbath afternoon, while he was holding his weekly lecture in the house of study, his two beloved sons died suddenly at home. The grief-stricken mother carried them to a room and covered them with a sheet. When Rabbi Meir returned after the evening services, he asked his wife, Beruriah, about the boys, whom he had missed in the synagogue. Instead of replying, she asked him to recite the special service marking the departure of the Sabbath. When he finished, she turned to her husband and said: "I have a question to ask you. Not long ago, some precious jewels were entrusted to my care. Now the owner has come to reclaim them. Shall I return them?" "But of course," said Rabbi Meir. "You know the law. Naturally they must be returned." His wife took him by the hand, led him to the bed, and drew back the sheet. Rabbi Meir burst into bitter weeping. "My sons! My sons!" he lamented. Then Beruriah reminded him tearfully, "Didn't you say that we must restore to the owner what he entrusted to our care? Our sons were the jewels which God left with us, and now their master has taken back His very own."

Death is the moment when God demands the return of His gifts. But it is not because He suddenly decided he wants to deprive us. It is because in His judgment His jewels deserve a better and more fitting setting.

My faith has taught me to appreciate life and to be prepared for death. To be ready and not to fear. To know that what follows is even better than what preceded. And to be wise enough to share the conviction of the Hasidic rabbi who, when asked on his death-bed how he was feeling, responded, "Almost well."

It is profoundly meaningful that we universally speak of the Angel of Death. If death is carried out by an Angel, its mission must be divinely ordained, and its purpose must be suffused with mercy, with infinite love, and with divine wisdom.

That is why, fully aware of my imminent mortality, I will, in the words of the 23rd Psalm, fear no evil—for Thou art with me.

SUGGESTED READINGS

Reincarnation: The Phoenix Fire Mystery—An East-West Dialogue on Death and Rebirth from the Worlds of Religion, Science, Psychology, Philosophy

Sylvia Cranston

This classic anthology offers ancient and modern perspectives on Job's question: "If a man die, shall he live again?" Spanning over five thousand years of world thought, the selections invite consideration of an idea that has found hospitality in the greatest minds of history.

You Have Been Here Before: A Psychologist Looks at Past Lives

Edith Fiore

The author's focus is on how events in our past lives influence our behaviors (even mental health!) in *this* lifetime.

Beyond the Ashes: Cases of Reincarnation from the Holocaust

Yonassan Gershom

Is it possible that people living today died in the Holocaust? Rabbi Yonassan Gershom presents compelling evidence that supports this seemingly impossible phenomenon. Based on the stories of people he counseled, the author sheds new light on the subject of reincarnation and the divinity of the human soul.

The Death of Death: Resurrection and Immortality

Neil Gillman

Gillman, a professor of Jewish philosophy at the Jewish Theological Seminary, takes on death, at least as an intellectual exercise, and offers an interesting survey of the topic in the context of Jewish religious thought. Starting with the Garden of Eden, Gillman examines the various ways Judaism, a religion often thought to be concerned exclusively with living, has dealt with the matter of dying.

Surviving Death: A Journalist Investigates Evidence for an Afterlife

Leslie Kean

With a keen eye and a no-nonsense approach, investigative journalist Leslie Kean explores what the actual data tell us about the question of survival past death. Examining many phenomena and case studies with penetrating depth and insight, Kean lets the evidence speak for itself. She takes us on an engaging, personal, and transformative journey that challenges the skeptic and informs us all.

Death Is of Vital Importance: On Life, Death, and Life after Death

Elisabeth Kübler-Ross

Internationally known author Dr. Elisabeth Kübler-Ross wanted to study the possibility of an afterlife so she decided to review the near-death experiences of children. She did so because they would not have any preconceived ideas of what it should be like (i.e., the tunnel, the light at the end of the tunnel that has become a cliché). What she discovers in her study is remarkable and very comforting for anyone who is losing a loved one.

On Life after Death

Elisabeth Kübler-Ross

In this collection of inspirational essays, Kübler-Ross draws on her in-depth research of more than twenty thousand people who had near-death experiences, revealing the afterlife as a return to wholeness of spirit. With frank and compassionate advice for those dealing with terminal illness or the death of a loved one, *On Life after Death* offers a compelling message of hope to the living so that they may grow stronger from tragedy and live life to the fullest.

Epistle on Resurrection of the Dead

Moses Maimonides, translated and with commentary by Fred Rosner

One of Maimonides' classic works, the *Treatise on Resurrection* is an extended discussion of resurrection, the immortality of the soul, the mysteries of the Messianic Age, and the World to Come. The *Treatise on Resurrection* was controversial in its day for its departure from accepted Jewish theology. Despite opposition to his ideas, Maimonides defended his view with skill and confidence. Dr. Fred Rosner's notes provide the background necessary to fully understand Maimonides's position, and his translation is an articulate rendering of this influential text, which validates resurrection as one of the cardinal principles of Judaism.

God and the Big Bang: Discovering Harmony between Science and Spirituality

Daniel Matt

In the past, the conversation between religion and science often turned bitter and acrimonious because neither camp was willing to listen to the other's ideas. In recent years, however, as both scientists and religious thinkers have demonstrated, the congruence between the two worldviews runs far deeper than either is sometimes willing to admit. In this book, Matt, a professor of Jewish spirituality, explores the connections between Jewish mysticism and the cosmological theory of the Big Bang.

Life after Life

Raymond Moody

Raymond Moody is the bestselling author of eleven books, which have sold over 20 million copies. His seminal work, *Life after Life*, has completely changed the way we view death and dying and has sold over 13 million copies worldwide. In this fascinating book, Dr. Moody reveals his groundbreaking study of more than one hundred people who experienced "clinical death"—and were revived. Their amazing testimonies and surprising descriptions of "death" and "beyond" are so strikingly similar, so vivid, and so overwhelmingly positive that they have changed the way we view life, death, and the spiritual hereafter.

Closer to the Light

Melvin Morse

In hundreds of interviews with children who had once been declared clinically dead, Dr. Morse found that children, too young to have absorbed our adult views and ideas of death, share firsthand accounts of out-of-body travel, telepathic communication, and encounters with dead friends and relatives. Finally illuminating what it is like to die, here is proof that there is that elusive "something" that survives "bodily death."

Transformed by the Light

Melvin Morse and Paul Perry

Written by bestselling authors Dr. Melvin Morse and Paul Perry, *Transformed by the Light* proves that those who return from the brink of death are profoundly changed for the better—spiritually and physically—for the rest of their lives, and that these documented changes provide deeper peace and understanding for all who come in contact with them.

Jewish Views of the Afterlife

Simchah Rafael and Zalman Schachter-Shalomi

This book traces, in a synoptic style, four thousand years of Jewish thought on the afterlife by investigating pertinent sacred texts produced in each era. From the Bible, Apocrypha, rabbinic literature, medieval philosophy, medieval Midrash, Kabbalah, and Hasidism, the reader learns how Judaism conceived of the fate of the individual after death throughout Jewish history.

What Happens after I Die: Jewish Views of Life after Death

Rifat Sonsino and Daniel B. Syme

The authors offer a wide spectrum of Jewish responses to the question of life after death. Classical answers are drawn from traditional Jewish literature. Modern Jewish thinkers, from all denominations in the Jewish community, add their personal notions of life after death.

Does the Soul Survive? A Jewish Journey to Belief in Afterlife, Past Lives and Living with Purpose

Elie Kaplan Spitz

Does the Soul Survive? combines journalistic reporting, scholarly biblical reading, and the probing self-examination of memoir in recounting the author's journey from skepticism to belief regarding life after death. Rabbi Spitz, who teaches the philosophy of law at the University of Judaism, carefully describes traditional Jewish views of the afterlife and fearlessly explores the many challenges to those views arising in parapsychology—including near-death experiences, reincarnation, and spirit mediums. In the end, Spitz makes a cogent argument that belief in the afterlife is not, as has often been argued, incompatible with Jewish tradition.

Children Who Remember Previous Lives: A Question of Reincarnation

Ian Stevenson

This work gives an overview of the history of the belief in and evidence for reincarnation. Representative cases of children, research methods used, analyses of the cases and of variations due to different cultures, and the explanatory value of the idea of reincarnation for some unsolved problems in psychology and medicine are reviewed. New material relating to birthmarks and birth defects, independent replication studies with a critique of criticisms, and recent developments in genetic study are included.

Many Lives, Many Masters

Brian Weiss

The classic bestseller on a true case of past-life trauma and past-life therapy from author and psychotherapist Dr. Brian Weiss. Psychiatry and metaphysics blend together in this fascinating book based on an actual case history. Dr. Weiss, who was once firmly entrenched in a clinical approach to psychiatry, finds himself reluctantly drawn into past-life therapy when a hypnotized client suddenly reveals details of her previous lives.

Joseph Karo, Lawyer and Mystic

R. J. Werblowsky

Joseph Karo (1488–1575) was one of the greatest figures of rabbinic Judaism and the author of the *Shulhan Arukh*, the standard code of Jewish Law. Like many other rabbinic ascetics who would write on talmudic or kabbalistic subjects yet carefully conceal their intimate mystical experiences, Karo left a diary, *Maggid Mesha-rim*, recording the messages that he received from a celestial mentor.

INDEX

values, 13; affirmation of, 86; jewels
    and, 87
the Vatican, 108–109

wealth, 25; spirituality and, 80
Weiss, Brian, 113–114
the West, 78
Whitman, Walt, 130
wisdom, 75; experience and, 21, 119

wishes, 19–25
witness, 130; testimony of, 35–41
worlds, 52
World War II, 104

youth, 66; death of, 33, 81

Zohar, 115

ABOUT THE AUTHOR

Rabbi Benjamin Blech is an internationally recognized educator, religious leader, author, and lecturer. He is the author of thirteen books, including his latest *New York Times* bestseller, *The Sistine Secrets: Michelangelo's Forbidden Messages in the Heart of the Vatican*, translated into fifteen languages and published in twenty-five countries. He has written for the *New York Times*, *The Wall Street Journal*, *Newsweek* and other major periodicals, in addition to a wide and varied number of scholarly publications. A recipient of the American Educator of the Year Award, he is professor of Jewish studies at Yeshiva University. He lives in New York City with his wife, Elaine.